AF255649

Energy Healing

How to Balance Your Chakras and Aura to Raise Positive Vibrations and Restore Inner Peace

Your Free Gift
(only available for a limited time)

Thanks for getting this book! If you want to learn more about various spirituality topics, then join Mari Silva's community and get a free guided meditation MP3 for awakening your third eye. This guided meditation mp3 is designed to open and strengthen ones third eye so you can experience a higher state of consciousness. Simply visit the link below the image to get started.

https://spiritualityspot.com/meditation

Or, Scan the QR code!

Table of Contents

INTRODUCTION 1

CHAPTER 1: WHAT IS ENERGY HEALING? 3

CHAPTER 2: CHAKRAS AND THEIR ENERGIES 15

CHAPTER 3: THE AURA EXPLAINED..31

CHAPTER 4: TOOLS AND TECHNIQUES FOR EASY ENERGY
HEALING 43

CHAPTER 5: HEALING MEDITATIONS AND BREATHWORK 57

CHAPTER 6: VISUALIZATIONS AND JOURNEYS FOR INNER
PEACE...67

CHAPTER 7: SHIELDING YOUR ENERGY FROM NEGATIVITY 77

CHAPTER 8: DAILY ENERGY PRACTICES FOR A FULFILLING LIFE 86

ENERGY HEALING GLOSSARY FOR QUICK REFERENCE...........................95

CONCLUSION 103

HERE'S ANOTHER BOOK BY MARI SILVA THAT YOU MIGHT
LIKE 106

YOUR FREE GIFT (ONLY AVAILABLE FOR A LIMITED TIME) 107

REFERENCES...108

IMAGE SOURCES 112

Introduction

In practical terms, the different obstacles and curveballs that life might throw your way will require practical solutions at various levels of effort and difficulty. However, not every battle is exclusively practical or external. Sometimes, helping yourself means fighting an inner battle before you can put yourself in a position to take on external challenges. Winning on this internal front is the way to fortify yourself spiritually and mentally, which will make all of your other battles easier at the least or change your whole life at the most.

There is a whole hidden world within you, in everyone else, and between the seams of what makes up this reality. This is a world of unseen energies and vibrations that might not be immediately apparent to the five senses, but these forces directly impact many things in the physical world and, ultimately, your own life.

Your energy is an essential force that keeps you going and can determine your physical state, feelings, thoughts, and even the kind of fortune you attract.

Like your body, your personal energy field can be prone to complications and issues that need to be addressed. Usually interpreted through concepts such as the chakra system or the aura, this energy can be healed if it has incurred damage. Healing your energy is a spiritual undertaking, but it involves a lot of practical steps that address the problem at the levels of chakras, aura, and other layers. Healing your chakras, aura, and overall energy might seem like a distant or abstract concept at first glance, but this book will show you that it's much more than that.

In this book, you'll be privy to a detailed yet comprehensive study of what your energy and aura are, how they work, what can go wrong, and how you can heal your energy.

Whether you're a complete beginner or have dabbled in the topic of energy healing, this book will teach you everything you need to know to embark on your healing journey and fulfill your spiritual, mental, and physical potential.

Your energy healing journey will be a trek of self-realization and actualization that leads to harmony on spiritual, mental, and emotional levels.

To understand your energy body, aura, and chakra system is to grasp spiritual concepts, but it also entails plenty of practical techniques that you'll learn about in this book. This comprehensive guide will ensure a wealth of knowledge if you're a beginner or serve as a point of reference if you're experienced, relying on meditation, visualization, energy shielding, and much more. With this information, you'll achieve balance, harmony, and inner peace that will enable you to prosper and improve your well-being in all the other areas of your life.

Chapter 1: What Is Energy Healing?

Learning to heal your energy begins with understanding the core concepts of energy healing, such as the meaning of energy itself and how it manifests. Before you delve into actionable energy healing techniques, you must build up a solid foundation of knowledge about this invisible world of energy and how it affects your daily life. Understanding what it is and what it does will help you see the potential problems that can emerge and identify which of these problems might apply to you.

You need to understand the implications of the invisible world and how you can utilize it to your advantage.[1]

This opening chapter will explore the basics of these concepts with enough depth to prepare you to delve deeper. It will describe the ways in which the state of your energy has real-world effects that you notice in your daily life. Most of all, this introductory chapter will ensure that you fully grasp what energy healing is and what benefits you can expect from pursuing it. You'll also gain some insight into the history of energy healing in its various cultural and civilizational contexts, as well as some starting practical tips to help you tune into your energy.

Energy and the Energy Body

In broad spiritual contexts, the word "energy" can contain many meanings. The simplest way to look at your energy is to consider it a force of vitality and life that permeates the entirety of your being.

Just as electricity powers a network of devices plugged into a broader system, so does the energy of life flow through the entire universe. You and every other creature and object are conduits to that vital force that flows through the universe. As a part of that network, you possess your own charge or share of that energy, which affects your mind, body, and spirit.

Your personal energy also has certain parts that work together to make sure that the energy flows freely and smoothly. When certain aspects of your energy fall out of balance or become blocked for any reason, the flow will become interrupted and diminished. A weakening, disturbance, or corruption of the energy that's supposed to flow through you can manifest in many ways. Lethargy, emotional problems, instability, stress, depression, discomfort, physical ailments, and much more can all be the result of complications with your energy.

A popular way of understanding your energy is through chakras, a string of energy nodes that govern different aspects of your being. You'll learn more about the chakras in later chapters, but the crux of the idea is that these points of concentration in your energy must be in balance and harmony. When they're working as they should, the chakras enable a free flow of energy that ensures you are operating at an optimal level in terms of health, emotions, and mental processes.

You can also view your energy as a field, typically called an aura. A related and somewhat different interpretation is something called the energy body. Starting with the understanding that there is a universal vital energy that connects all things in the universe, you can consider your energy body to be one node in that system of energy. Different traditions offer various breakdowns of this concept, but the energy body is generally understood to consist of five main layers, which are also known as the subtle bodies.

If the chakras are concentration points where your energy converges into unique centers that affect you in different ways, then the energy body is the entirety of your energy. Chakras can also be considered as communication nodes that transfer your energy between your physical and energy bodies. These concepts can be a lot to handle at first glance if you're a beginner, but the following chapters will gradually bring the teachings closer to your grasp.

Aspects and Interpretations

The understanding of the broader concept of energy can be broken down into a few components and related concepts that will make it easier to grasp. Vibrational frequencies are one of the most important aspects of vital energy both in yourself and your environment. Other concepts that can relate to your energy include bioelectricity, quantum energy, and electromagnetic fields. Different interpretations of energy healing ascribe various levels of importance to each of these factors, but the general consensus is that they can all have at least some effect on your general wellness and happiness.

First and foremost, everything in the universe has its unique vibrational frequency, including objects and living creatures. Your energy body vibrates at a certain frequency, which can be altered by internal or external stimuli. Measured in Hertz, your frequency simply represents how fast your energy vibrates. Applied at a higher, more abstract level, the idea of vibration can be attached to things like thoughts and feelings as well. Love and malice, for instance, vibrate at vastly different frequencies, as do the energy and physical bodies of individuals with different personalities and mentalities.

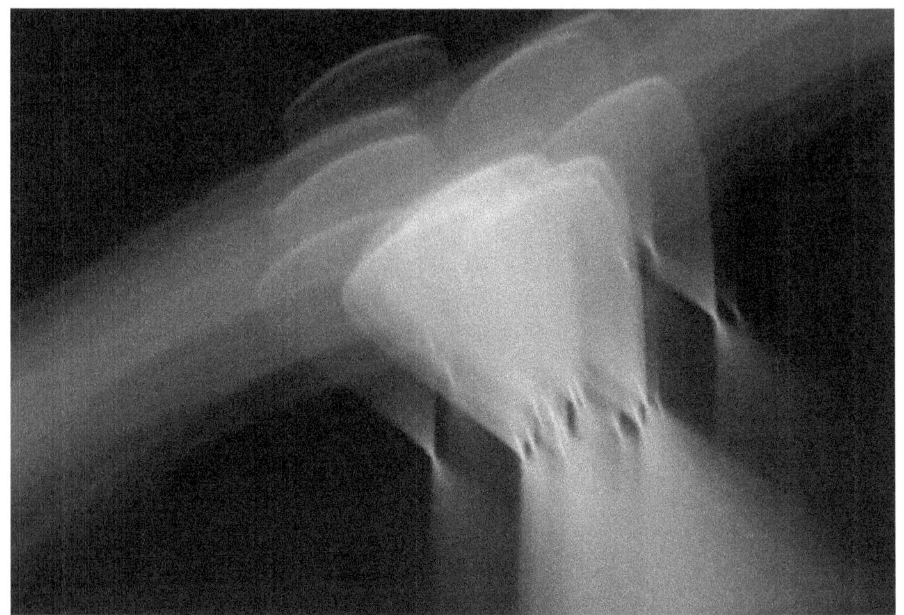

Everything in the universe has its own vibrational frequency.[2]

Frequencies that relate specifically to your energy body or field can also be called spiritual vibration. The spiritual practices you engage in, the thoughts you think, and the emotions you feel will all affect your vibration in this context. Higher frequencies are generally associated with positive feelings and spiritual growth. This is why sound therapy is an increasingly popular approach in modern energy healing, borrowing aspects of both modern science and traditional views on energy healing.

Sound therapy or sound healing is sometimes classified as vibrational medicine. It's an energy healing technique in its essence, but its methodology focuses primarily on stimuli that can be observed with regular senses.

In sound therapy, specific sound waves are utilized for their therapeutic effects in a holistic approach that alleviates physical ailments and promotes peace of mind and spiritual growth. This is because sound can have a profound effect on your energy field, being able to disrupt or balance your vibrational frequency. While sound therapy has seen some recent growth in popularity thanks to modern methods, it's actually not an entirely new concept. Things like singing bowls and chants have been used in energy work and healing for thousands of years. This is especially apparent in Eastern traditions that rely heavily on chants or, more specifically, mantras.

Apart from vibrational frequencies, you should also be mindful of bioelectricity, which projects an energy field around living creatures and emanates directly from cells. Bioelectricity and electromagnetism in the context of energy work and spiritual practice are often associated with the aura, which will be discussed at length later on. The aura is a more recent concept that brings together a lot of the aforementioned terms and ideas into a singular concept that makes your energy easier to understand in daily practice.

Quantum energy and quantum healing are also worth mentioning because their adjacent teachings often refer to energy and vibrations. This loose body of spiritual and esoteric practice focuses on quantum phenomena, which are believed to have extensive control over the health and well-being of living creatures. Quantum healing is a more recent practice that diverges considerably from traditional approaches to energy healing, often considered as its own branch of alternative medicine.

The Purpose and Benefits of Energy Healing

The goal of energy healing is primarily to eliminate problems in your own energy, among other issues. Other practices, such as the many spiritual protection methods, are more focused on protecting one's energy from malign outside influences, but healing has an inward orientation. Energy healing is all about unblocking and cleansing your energy itself and, sometimes, focusing on physical ailments through energy work. The latter is commonly encountered in traditional medicine and similar practices that bridge the gap between the physical and the spiritual.

Whereas physical healing zeroes in on a physical problem and its physiological symptoms and causes, energy healing represents a holistic approach. This is because most traditions that deal with energy healing ascribe equal importance to the matters of the mind, body, and spirit. These three core aspects of your being cover every layer of what it is to be human, which is why energy healing has such a broad spectrum of applications. As a result, the potential benefits are immense and far-reaching.

Physical Benefits

One of the common symptoms of a clogged or otherwise diminished flow of energy is stress, which is a well-known culprit in many other complications. Apart from being mentally debilitating, stress has very real consequences for your physical health as well. It can weaken your immunity, affect your appetite, disrupt your sleep cycle, strain your heart, and much more. That's why one of the greatest benefits of energy healing is that it relieves stress.

Energy healing can also help you reduce or eliminate tension in a broader sense, including physical tension. Blockages in your energy can often cause you to tense up and feel stiff, even if you don't live a particularly unhealthy lifestyle. By extension, a reduction in tension and stress will have tremendous benefits for the quality of your sleep. Getting sufficient and uninterrupted sleep is one of the most important ingredients in your health, so if your potential sleep issues are alleviated via energy healing, the benefits will be immense across the board.

Because of its positive effects on your sleep and all the other physical benefits, energy healing can also provide a powerful boost to your immune system. If your energy is clear and free-flowing, this alone can improve your immunity, but it's the overall reduction in stress and your newfound mental and physical balance that will take your resilience to a new level.

Emotional Benefits

The benefits mentioned earlier will also translate to your emotional well-being. The healthier and more balanced you feel physically, the more stable your emotional state will be as well. Energy healing also affects your emotional state directly, helping you unblock yourself emotionally, open up to life, and understand your own needs with more clarity.

Since energy healing involves quite a bit of meditation, it will inevitably reduce your anxiety levels. With a newfound sense of emotional clarity and fortitude, you might find that the things that once rattled you are no longer as frightening. When your energy is healthy and balanced, you'll gain a new perspective on the factors of stress and fear in your life, which applies to relationships, professional life, and much more.

You'll also find it easier to articulate your emotions, which is crucial if you are to effectively communicate your needs to the people in your life and operate on a level playing field. Needless to say, the benefits to your emotional well-being will also reverberate positively in the relationships that are important to you. A lot of the problems in personal relationships stem from emotional blocks and the resulting miscommunication, all of which can be mended through energy work.

Spiritual Benefits

Last but not least, energy healing and energy work, in general, will elevate your spirituality to new heights. To be healthy and balanced in spirit might be less tangible and immediately apparent than your physical and emotional health, but this doesn't make spirituality less important. When your energy is balanced, you will develop a higher level of self-awareness and become more intuitive.

This means knowing yourself while also being able to trust your gut, which is connected not just to better outcomes but confidence as well. If you can trust your intuition and see to the gist of things with the proverbial third eye, you'll become more assertive and proactive and less fearful and apprehensive. Energy healing will tune you into your higher self, expand your consciousness, and bring you closer to divinity.

Being of sound spirit will make your place in the universe clearer and more comforting, fostering a sense of interconnectedness and belonging. This kind of self-realization is essential if you are to understand your weaknesses and unlock your hidden strengths. Spirituality will give you peace of mind and put things in perspective, making you more stable and resilient overall. To heal your energy is to unclog the channels of your spirituality and improve your communication with your true self, the universe, and everyone around you.

A Historical Practice

As a holistic approach to wellness, energy healing has a long and well-established history with contributions from various cultures across the world. For thousands of years, different civilizations have been coming up with their own interpretations of the underlying energies that keep living creatures in motion and balance. Just as importantly, these traditions have made efforts to tune into this energy, harness it, and use it for healing, other forms of self-betterment, and connecting with the divine.

Energy is something that has been studied across generations and cultures.[8]

Hindu traditions refer to this life force as Prana, traditional Chinese medicine and spirituality call it Qi, and indigenous cultures across the Americas have their own views on the matter. Many other cultures across time and space have used different names and interpretations, but all of them generally refer to a very similar concept. The sense that an overarching force of life permeates all of existence seems to be ubiquitous, spontaneously emerging in the collective consciousness of communities that had no historical contact with each other.

The Hindu concept of Prana summarizes the idea quite effectively. According to numerous traditions in the Indian subcontinent, Prana is an ethereal form of energy that exists beyond the scope of your senses, yet it flows through every layer of the universe. It's an energetic essence found in all things, including you, animals, inanimate objects, matter, and much more. Throughout history and in modern times, the concept of Prana has played a key role in traditional medicine like Ayurveda, yogic practices from across the East, martial arts, and meditation.

Practiced in ancient Egypt, China, India, and many other locales, energy healing has traditionally been intertwined with religious practice and faith. Ancient Egyptians ascribed sacred meaning and power to symbols, amulets, and other aspects of their polytheistic belief system. The divine power contained in symbols was worshiped in a religious sense but also associated with healing.

Ancient Chinese traditions place a particularly high emphasis on healing, as exemplified by Qigong and the overall intricate system of traditional Chinese medicine that remains popular to this day. Qi, the traditional Chinese term for the Prana-like vital force found in all living things, makes direct reference to "breath" in its literal translation. It's also translated as "air" or "vapor," but it can take on more intricate meanings in looser translation, all of which refer to energy and vitality in some way. The association of this concept with breath is noteworthy because breathing is one of the core aspects of energy healing, meditation, and all sorts of other energy work.

Historically, Chinese views on energy healing have emphasized the guided flow of energy through a person's body to harness its healing power. For well over two millennia, traditional Chinese medicine has relied on a holistic approach that tends to the mind, body, and spirit with equal commitment. These practices have evolved significantly over time and carried over into the present day as holistic health approaches such as acupuncture, Reiki, sound therapy, and other approaches.

Reiki was also spawned from Eastern traditions, emerging in Japan in the early 20th century and making its way to the United States in the 1970s. Like the ancient practices it was inspired by, Reiki postulates the existence of a universal force of life, much like Qi and Prana. The teachings of Reiki focus on channeling this energy in a deliberate manner to encourage various healing processes in the human body. It's usually carried out by a trained Reiki expert who is well-versed in recognizing and manipulating energy flows via touch or a hands-off technique that seeks to achieve energetic balance in a patient.

There are a number of other modern energy healing techniques that draw on long-standing traditions in combination with contemporary scientific understanding. Apart from sound therapy, popular methods include crystal healing, quantum healing, and other techniques. The millennia have given rise to countless interpretations and schools of thought regarding energy healing, and new methods continue to emerge to this day. As different as some of these techniques might seem, they essentially all rely on the same principle. The goal is – and has always been – to affect an individual's energy field and flow in a way that promotes the wellness of mind, body, and soul.

Getting in Touch with Your Energy

On the practical side of all this, the first step is to become aware of your energy and learn how to sense it. Feeling its presence and observing it as clearly as the five senses allow will vastly improve your subsequent meditations, visualization, and other practices that are essential in energy healing. Described below are a few basic exercises and tips that will help you notice your energy through practical steps, particularly in regard to breathing.

The General Sensing of Energy

In great part, sensing your energy is an exercise in visualization and intense mental focus. You can try to sense energy in many ways, and whichever one you find most conducive to your visualization will do the trick for you. The general rule across methods is that you first want to get as comfortable as possible, which will allow you to focus on the exercise. Whether you choose to stand or sit doesn't matter too much as long as it allows you to be fully comfortable.

A common approach to sensing energy revolves around visualizing and noticing sensations between your palms. The first step is to relax, so once you've assumed a comfortable position, begin by focusing on your breathing. Take three deep, slow breaths to maximize your oxygen intake and energize your body, and repeat this if you need more time. Once you're feeling relaxed enough, place your hands in front of your body and have your palms facing each other.

Shift your focus to the surfaces of your palms and the empty space between them, trying to notice any sensations you might feel. To bolster your sensitivity to any energy flowing between your palms, try rubbing your hands together for a while and then separate the palms again. Repeat this process multiple times, each time placing your palms further away from each other. Visualize an invisible exchange of energy between your hands and focus your mind on physical sensations. With enough focus and effort, you should be able to feel some sensations even when your hands are quite far apart.

Full Breathing Exercise

Breathing plays a major part in any effort to feel your energy or encourage its flow. Your breathing pattern and the physical sensation of air coursing through your respiratory system are powerful objects for meditative focus, as you'll learn later on. For the moment, consider breathing as a way to simply feel the energy of life entering and circulating through your body. This is a basic exercise that's meant to establish a foundation for more complex practices by getting you in touch with the energy within you and the world around you.

Find a quiet place in your home and sit down comfortably, keeping your feet on the floor. The first step is to simply notice your breathing and act as an observer. Spend a little time contemplating the pattern and depth of your breathing and the feeling of the air entering your body and filling up your lungs. Once you're fully aware of your breathing, start to breathe deeper while keeping it slow and gentle.

Observe the ways in which your chest and abdomen move and work as you breathe. Visualize a balloon in the center of your body filling up when you inhale and emptying as you exhale. Try to think of this balloon as a storage compartment that accumulates the life force contained in each breath of air. Take at least three of these contemplative breaths while trying your best to form a mental connection between the air that courses through your body and the energy that enters in this manner.

Belly Breathing

When you breathe correctly, important things occur in your abdominal area. Diaphragmatic or belly breathing is an excellent way to get in tune with your energy and disseminate it throughout your body more effectively. More than that, using your diaphragm is the correct way to breathe and get the most oxygen out of each breath. The diaphragm is an important muscle situated just under the lungs, so when it is engaged during breathing, it contracts as you inhale and allows more room for your lungs to expand. A lot of people tend to lose their innate habit of diaphragmatic breathing as they age, relying solely on chest breathing. This makes breathing shallower and less energizing.

Belly breathing comes from focusing on your breath in your stomach area.‘

To exercise belly breathing, all you have to do is lie down comfortably and make yourself flat. Begin by positioning one hand on your upper chest and the other on your abdomen below the ribs, and then start inhaling slowly but deeply through your nose. As you pull the air in, try to direct it downward and toward your abdomen. As you inhale and engage your diaphragm, the hand that's on your belly should begin to rise. When it's time to exhale, gently squeeze your abdominal muscles, purse your lips, and push the air out. As you exhale, your hand should come back down.

Assuming that you normally don't breathe this way, enough practice should rekindle the old healthy habit. Belly breathing is the deepest and maximal mode of breathing with considerable health benefits. It's also a great way to sense how your body becomes energized as the air fills you up completely and makes its way to the very core of your body. The exercise will also work in a seated position if this position allows you to bend your knees and relax your upper body, especially the shoulders, neck, and head. Each exercise doesn't have to last more than ten minutes and should ideally be conducted multiple times throughout your day.

Chapter 2: Chakras and Their Energies

Now that you have a basic, generalized idea of what energy is and what it does, you can begin delving deeper into some of the individual aspects and properties of your energy. A holistic understanding of energy is necessary if you are to engage in effective energy healing, so you have to get a grasp on its individual parts.

The Chakra system is a longstanding concept in energy work.[5]

One such part is the chakra system, which is one of the most established and long-standing concepts in energy work. This will be another foundational chapter, focusing specifically on providing you with an understanding of how your chakras play a key role in the management and alignment of your energy. It will teach you the details of all the components and functions of the chakras system while also highlighting the ways in which the chakras affect your physical, emotional, and spiritual states.

Chakras 101

Usually represented symbolically as spinning wheels in illustrations, the chakras are best described as vortexes of energy strung along your body in a particular order. Every chakra is special and has a clearly defined nature, position, role, influence, and much more. Each chakra governs specific aspects of your physical and emotional well-being, and all the chakras combined are instrumental in your overall spiritual health and development. While the chakras are distinct in many ways, they are all interconnected in a system that must be kept in perfect harmony to allow your energy to flow freely through each part of that system.

The concept of chakras is fairly broad, and it has a long history in the traditions of the East, originating in the Indian subcontinent. For thousands of years, various interpretations and traditions have emerged, sometimes diverging in their understanding of how chakras work, especially regarding their number. The overall and most established view is that these focal points of energy are places of convergence for your energy. In most widespread practices, there are seven of them arranged mostly along the spine. The chakras are sometimes also seen as nodes of communication that bridge the gap between your physical and energy body.

These seven spinning wheels of energy begin at the base of your spinal column and ascend, one after the other, to the top of your head. According to most Hindu teachings, the chakras feed into each other as the vital energy of Prana flows right through them. When the chakras are balanced and clear, Prana will flow smoothly and enter every layer or subtle body of your energy body, energizing you physically, mentally, and spiritually. The chakras begin with the so-called root chakra around your tailbone, ending with the crown chakra, which sits on top of your head.

The word itself comes from Sanskrit and is usually translated as "circle," "wheel," and sometimes "cycle." The ancient belief in the chakra system is deeply ingrained in all manner of Eastern spiritual practices and, increasingly, across the rest of the world. However, many traditions, especially those in the Indian subcontinent, place special emphasis on the role of chakras in traditional medicine. Because of their individual positions and associations with the surrounding parts of the body, the chakras are seen as directly connected with things like organs. Traditionally, ailments in specific organs or parts were seen as mere symptoms of a spiritual, energetic problem in a particular chakra, not just a physical issue.

Beyond health, some chakras are connected to things like physical strength, intellect, speech, passion, various character traits, and much more. In the most holistic view, working on your chakras is a way to improve all facets of who you are as a person and as a physical entity. Attaining wisdom, being creative, connecting with divinity, finding passion, and the way you treat or attract other people are only some of the things that your chakras can affect.

In the past millennium, the concept of chakras has become notably entrenched in both Hinduism and Buddhism, especially those parts that focus on meditation, yoga, and traditional medicine. Chakras are a major focal point in the medical traditions of Ayurveda, with the goal of opening the chakras and achieving energy balance in a holistic approach. Ayurveda traditions use a combination of meditation, herbs, and other approaches for this purpose. On the other hand, various yogic techniques emphasize breath as the primary tool for opening and balancing the chakras. Yoga aims to facilitate the movement of life energy through the body, meaning the chakras, by utilizing the power of breathing and altering it as needed.

It took a while for the concept of chakras to proliferate across the West, with the greatest breakthroughs occurring in the second half of the 20th century. While Indian religions have long used chakras in many mainline religious and medicinal practices, the idea came to the West mostly through alternative conceptions of spirituality and healing. The popularity of yoga in recent times has done a lot to bring the idea of chakras much closer to the general populace. Over time, chakras in the West have gone beyond spiritual practice and entered the fields of psychology and even medicine, at least as a way to complement more mainstream approaches to ailments.

Getting vital energy to flow through the chakras unimpeded is usually referred to as balancing or alignment. Chakras become problematic when they're either blocked for any reason or stressed by an extreme concentration of energy. When this happens, a chakra is considered to be out of balance, with symptoms following close behind. Aligning one's chakras can be done in a number of ways, with various traditions offering a number of different approaches. The end goal is not just for your energy to flow smoothly through your chakra system and circulate in your body but also to flow out and connect to the broader energy of the universe. These teachings postulate that your inner balance and your interconnectedness with the rest of the universe are equally important for your overall well-being.

Depending on what body of traditional teaching you turn to, you might choose to align your chakras through meditation, breathing exercises, various yoga techniques, Ayurveda, color therapy, crystal healing, or more modern approaches like Reiki. There are many techniques, but a lot of them have some common features, like visualization and an emphasis on breathing. However, in most of these techniques, chakra alignment is just one part of the puzzle. Even though chakras are essential to how your energy works, they are just one aspect of a broader system. Later chapters will delve into many techniques that will apply to chakra alignment, but you'll find that energy healing has broader positive implications for your spirituality and health.

The Seven Chakras

The following rundown will provide you with a comprehensive overview of all seven chakras, outlining their Sanskrit name, color, sound (chant or mantra), associated natural elements and body parts, and other details. The details describing each chakra are essential in meditation and visualization exercises because they'll give you plenty of material to help visualize the chakras.

Muladhara – Root Chakra

Root Chakra.[6]

Color: Red

Chant: Lam

Element: Earth

Location: Tailbone

Located at the base of the spine, the root chakra is your first chakra and represents all things related to grounding and stability. A healthy root chakra enables you to find your footing in the world and connect to it, feeling stability on the emotional, physical, and spiritual levels. The root chakra is also related to survival instincts, dependency, ambition, and more. In relation to your energy, you can see the root chakra as your foundation, with the same implications that the stability of the foundation has for any structure. The feeling of stability that a balanced root chakra provides is essential to feelings of security and safety, so it plays an important role in how you respond to stress.

Svadhishthana – Sacral Chakra

Sacral Chakra.[7]

Color: Orange

Chant: Vam

Element: Water

Location: Lower abdomen, below the navel

The sacral chakra is connected to things like sexuality, creativity, and the overall sense of pleasure in life. In traditional Indian medicine, a blocked sacral chakra can lead to reproductive problems, urinary infections, and problems with your lower back. The energy of this chakra is the emotional driver of self-worth in various life pursuits, particularly those related to pleasure and creativity. It affects your ability to derive pleasure from things and feel emotionally satisfied. As an energetic center of your sexuality and creativity, the sacral chakra has a profound effect on your ability to find joy in life. A balanced sacral chakra is instrumental in the pursuit of life fulfillment.

Manipura – Solar Plexus Chakra

Solar Plexus Chakra.[8]

Color: Yellow

Chant: Ram

Element: Fire

Location: Upper abdomen, between navel and rib cage

The solar plexus chakra is responsible for providing you with a sense of confidence and self-esteem. By extension, it's sometimes also associated with individuality and power. This is where you get your will to charge forward, take action, and commit to tasks. People with a blocked solar plexus chakra can become marred by indecision and anger management problems. Because it's connected to self-esteem, an imbalanced Manipura can also turn you egotistical or, conversely, destroy your self-esteem. Digestive issues are common symptoms of a blocked Manipura on the physical side. With a balanced solar plexus chakra, you'll be able to form a healthy self-image and take life's challenges in stride.

Anahata – Heart Chakra

Heart Chakra.[9]

Color: Green

Chant: Yam

Element: Air

Location: Central chest

While the root chakra is often considered the foundational chakra, the Anahata is seen as the central chakra. Apart from being an energy focal point in the same way as the others, your heart chakra can also be seen as a point of convergence for your physical and spiritual qualities. As the place where the tangible and intangible meet, the heart chakra is a powerful energy vortex that has a lot to do with love and compassion. Because energy is both projected and attracted, a balanced heart chakra will ensure that your life is filled with love and compassion in both directions. This chakra fosters your ability to have love for others while also attracting the same from other people. It also gives you the strength to forgive and the selflessness to serve others.

Vishuddha – Throat Chakra

Throat Chakra.[10]

Color: Blue

Chant: Ham

Element: Space or ether

Location: Throat

The throat chakra governs communication in the broadest sense. An imbalanced throat chakra can make it difficult for you to communicate effectively, which will inevitably affect relationships and your ability to express your needs or set boundaries. Certain interpretations hold that this fifth chakra marks the beginning of your spiritual chakras. This means that the three final chakras are more closely related to your spirituality than the other chakras, whose physical qualities are more pronounced. Since communication is a two-way street, a balanced throat chakra will also ensure that you'll understand others more easily and truly listen to their expressions.

Third Eye Chakra.[11]

Color: Indigo

Chant: Om

Element: None, sometimes light

Location: Forehead or brow, between the eyes

As one of the more famous chakras, the Ajna governs intuition, imagination, and psychic abilities, among other things. The third eye chakra also powers your ability to observe the big picture, notice patterns, and see right through to the essence of all things. It also allows you to see the connections between things more clearly, including your own connection to the world and the universe. This chakra also plays a part in wisdom and higher spirituality. When the Ajna is running at optimal energy, you're able to get more out of your meditation and any other spiritual practice. You'll also have no trouble trusting your intuition and venturing beyond your comfort zone.

Crown Chakra.[12]

Color: Violet, sometimes white

Chant: Ah

Element: None

Location: Top of the head

As the highest and final one, your crown chakra is what enables enlightenment and the utmost spiritual growth. It's the node through which your energy communicates with divinity and flows out into the higher network. Spiritual and energy work focuses on the crown chakra, which is how a human soul becomes one with the universe and reaches its spiritual peak. A blockage in this chakra can trigger profound feelings of disconnect and energetic diminishment. Seasoned spiritualists and masters of meditation and yoga often commit a lot of time to work on their crown chakra to fully open it and attain enlightenment.

When a chakra is in balance and working optimally, it will govern its particular area unimpeded, granting you the benefits of its ideal energy flow. If any of your chakras become blocked, you will be able to see certain signs. Like any physical ailment, a problem with your chakras will have symptoms that can affect your health in the broadest terms.

Building on the information provided above, the chart below will give you a quick rundown of the effect each chakra can have in its balanced and imbalanced states, as well as some tips on how to begin to address the problem.

In combination with the information provided in the detailed breakdown of the chakras, you can use this chart for quick reference. These tips will mostly be of a practical nature and aimed at encouraging each chakra to develop. You'll learn about more complex spiritual techniques and energy work in later chapters.

Chakra	Balanced	Imbalanced	Balancing Tip
Muladhara	Stability, positivity, security, confidence, strength, independence, and feeling energized.	Instability, a lack of firm footing, feelings of purposelessness, insecurity, frustration, fear, and a lack of ambition. Physical symptoms like lower back pain or issues with the colon and bladder.	Grounding meditation and other energy work focused on the chakra. Physical exercise focusing on the root chakra's location.
Svadhishthana	Feeling happy, satisfied, intuitive, compassionate, and vibrant.	Impulsivity and uncontrollable emotions, lethargy, impeded creativity, and overindulgence in sexual thoughts.	Keeping your body in good shape and indulging your creative impulses.
Manipura	Easily focused, confident, productive, and energized.	Digestive issues, liver problems, or even diabetes. Perfectionism, emotional drain and depression, lack of self-esteem.	Observing a healthy diet, practicing yoga, and building your confidence.

Chakra	Balanced	Imbalanced	Balancing Tip
Anahata	Feeling optimistic, friendly, and easily motivated. Compassion and overall friendliness.	Anxiety, jealousy, envy, mood swings, fear, and a lack of trust.	Opening up, working on your relationships, and employing self-care.
Vishuddha	Ease of expression, creativity, and smooth communicatio n.	Shyness, communication issues, physical weakness, and difficulties with expression.	Developing your speaking skills, active listening, and finding expressive outlets to help you articulate.
Ajna	Spiritual and emotional vibrancy, courage, and a lack of attachment to the material.	Difficulty asserting yourself, risk-aversion, egotism, headaches, eye discomfort.	Pursuing wisdom, developing your intuition, and trusting your inner voice.
Sahastrara	Profound spirituality, tranquility, and clarity of thought.	Destructive tendencies, emotional confusion, frustration, and melancholy.	Deep meditation and spiritual journeying.

Scanning and Balancing Your Chakras

Apart from the more detailed and complex energy work that you'll learn about later, a few basic chakra-related exercises are worth noting that every beginner can pick up quickly.

These focus on three main goals, including sensing the presence of your chakras, scanning them for blockages or weaknesses, and trying to balance the problematic ones. The simple exercises described below, which rely in great part on visualization, will serve as a foundation for higher energy work that comes later.

Sensing the Chakras

While you can hardly feel your chakras in a physical sense, you can use visualization to conjure up a powerful image of a chakra's presence in your body by using all the details provided above. If you visualize effectively, you'll be able to zero in on sensations that will communicate the presence of a chakra with considerable clarity. Sensing your chakras simply means fostering an awareness that they're there, which will be the first step toward sensing their state as well.

As with most energy work and spiritual techniques, the initial portion of the exercise is to enter a state of relaxation. Assume a comfortable position by sitting in a chair with your feet flat on the floor and your hands positioned on your thighs. Make sure that your elbows are relaxed and subdue any stiffness you might notice anywhere on your body. Ideally, you should do this in a quiet, private space where you can remove all distractions from your immediate surroundings. For maximum comfort, you should wear soft, loose clothes that exert no pressure on your body.

Begin with a simple breathing exercise to relax yourself and focus your mind on everything you've learned about your chakras. When you're ready, bring your palms toward your body and try to sense your energy first, just as you've learned earlier. Focus on your energy and visualize its flow through your body. Shift your awareness to the first chakra at the base of your spine and visualize the flow of energy through the chakra. Fixate on any sensations you might feel at the location of the root chakra, and repeat the same steps for every other chakra in the correct order. Use as many specific identifying details as you can remember when visualizing your chakras to make the mental image more distinct. It's also a good idea to use a journal and write down any sensations and reactions you might have.

Scanning the Chakras

The simplest way to scan the state of your chakras is to read the symptoms, but many of the discussed signs can sometimes be brought on by causes other than chakra blockages. Another method is to get a professional chakra scan from an energy or yoga instructor. To assess your chakras with more confidence at home, you can engage in forms of visualization similar to those aimed at sensing the chakras.

You can sit or lie down as long as you're fully comfortable and able to relax your body and mind. Shut your eyes and start breathing slowly, fully, and gently as you begin visualizing the flow of energy from your root chakra to the top. Spend time visualizing each chakra as a circle in the chakra's associated color. Think of it as a ball of light or energy that can be opened and accessed. If you get any closed-eye visuals and notice the chakra's color, focus intently on it. For the root chakra, look for the color red, and once you've found the chakra, try to visualize yourself opening it.

The trick is to pick up on any emotional, mental, or physical sensations that might occur as you visualize the opening of a chakra. When you look inside a chakra, these sensations might suggest something about its state. The idea behind visualizing the opening of a chakra is to remove blockages and encourage energy to flow through. It will be up to you to interpret the intensity of the color you might see and combine that information with your sensations to determine how your chakras are doing. If you struggle to visualize a chakra's color, that might be because it's too weak and blocked.

Balancing the Chakras

Balancing your chakras can be done through the tips and advice covered earlier or through a whole range of techniques in energy healing, meditation, yoga, and much more.

Many yoga classes you might attend will emphasize the chakras and use them to improve your general well-being. Generally speaking, the most accessible and simplistic method of clearing your chakras is following a healthy lifestyle with plenty of exercise, yoga, and healthy food. For a more tailored approach to each chakra, you must attend to them individually. As an example, each chakra seems to have a preference for certain yoga poses, as listed below:

- **Muladhara** – Vrkshasana and Tadasana, respectively, are known as the tree pose and mountain pose.

- **Svadhishthana** – Kakasana and Trikonasana, also called the crow and triangle poses.

- **Manipura** – Paschimottanasana, Bhujangasana, and Dhanurasana, or the forward bend, cobra, and bow poses.

- **Anahata** – Ardha Setubandhasana and Matsyasana, known as the half-bridge and fish poses.

- **Vishuddha** – Sarvangasana and Halasana, translated as the shoulder stand and plow poses.

- **Ajna** – Shirshasana or the headstand.

- **Sahastrara** – Headstand also applies.

A simple visualization exercise can also help you promote balance among your chakras. Lie down and enter a state of relaxation, as in the other exercises, and begin sensing your energy. Try to visualize a column of healing white light above your head, descending from a powerful but benevolent outside source. As you draw breath, visualize yourself drawing that light closer to your head.

With your next breath, inhale and imagine that light entering through your crown chakra and passing on all the way to the root chakra. Visualize this light as an unstoppable force of life trying to break through any blockages as it passes through your chakras. Whenever you arrive at a certain chakra, regardless of the aim of your visualization exercise, remember to use the chakra's chant. Refer to the earlier detailed breakdown of the chakras and try to memorize each chakra's sound. Chanting these simple, vibrating sounds while meditating and visualizing will stimulate your chakras and encourage them to open up.

Chapter 3: The Aura Explained

Continuing along a trajectory similar to the last chapter, this one will focus on another essential concept in energy work: the aura.

In modern times, the aura is one of the most popular ways of interpreting and summarizing most things related to the energy field or body that every individual possesses. Just like the chakra system, your aura features multiple aspects that combine into a unified concept. Your aura reflects a lot about your physical, emotional, and spiritual state, which is why it's important to understand how it works and how to read it. This chapter will go into detail on what your aura is and how it works while also providing some practical advice on how to sense your aura and understand the symptoms of its potential weakness.

Understanding the concept of the aura will help you tap into its benefits.[18]

Definition

Because of its fame and prevalence across popular culture and spiritual practices, the concept of aura has attained a lot of meanings over the years.

The definition varies somewhat from one interpretation to another, but there is an overarching idea that describes the aura in comprehensive terms. One way to explain it is by stating that aura is an electromagnetic field that surrounds all living beings. You can also consider it as your spiritual fingerprint of sorts, as your aura is closely connected to your thoughts, emotions, spirit, and overall well-being.

The aura is important because it reflects a lot about the state of these aspects of your being. This means that your aura will react in different ways to internal changes and can provide important information that will assist in energy healing and many other self-care exercises.

Practical work regarding the aura consists of auric sensing or reading and the numerous ways in which the aura can be healed, strengthened, or shielded. There are schools of thought that believe that the aura can be observed with the right skill set and in certain conditions. In those approaches, the aura is read and analyzed based on things like color and intensity.

The concept of aura differs from things like Prana and the chakras in that it has emerged more recently, originating in the West. Nonetheless, the idea behind auras draws a lot of inspiration and knowledge from Eastern traditions that stretch back thousands of years. The term "aura" is sometimes used interchangeably with "energy body" in some circles, while others prefer to separate the two. There are several similarities, particularly the layered nature of these energy fields.

From the practical standpoint of a spiritually curious individual such as yourself, you should consider your aura as just another facet of your energy.

It's one more way to visualize your energy, analyze it, and heal it. The applicability of a lot of the techniques that you'll start learning about after this chapter will overlap across your chakras, aura, and other aspects of your energy balance. Your aura can also be seen as an energetic extension of the self, intimately connected to your current state and your innate traits and personality. The aura is also commonly mentioned in the techniques of spiritual protection because it can be vulnerable at times. The vulnerability can come from internal causes that make the aura weak or from negative external energy.

While a person's aura can be difficult to see directly, its presence can be quite strong and noticeable in other ways. The aura is usually at play in those situations when you feel like someone radiates a particularly positive or negative energy or when you seem to attract certain vibes or people. Auras can interact and have effects on one another, leaving lasting impressions and sensations. The easiest way to imagine your aura through a real-world example is to consider the way a magnet projects its magnetic field in its vicinity.

The gifted few who possess the psychic skills to see auras describe them as colorful, which is why discussions surrounding auras often reference a range of colors and their meanings. These colors can change depending on certain influences, particularly those that come from within you. The aura will also usually have a constant color that it tends to default to, which corresponds to personality. Based on all this, you can visualize your aura as similar to a magnetic field in nature but also luminous because of its color. It follows the contours of your body and is projected to a distance of at least a few inches. A more powerful and intense aura will naturally extend further, depending on the intensity of a person's energy and spiritual development.

The Aura's Layers

Traditions related to the concept of aura often describe it as consisting of multiple auric layers. There are seven primary layers to understand, each governing a particular dimension of your personality, body, energy, feelings, and much more. From you as the foundation, these layers are stacked on top of each other as they are projected to the outermost layer of your auric field. The seven layers are also sometimes referred to as the "bodies" of your aura, and each of them also corresponds to a chakra. Every layer reflects a particular aspect of the self, starting with the physical.

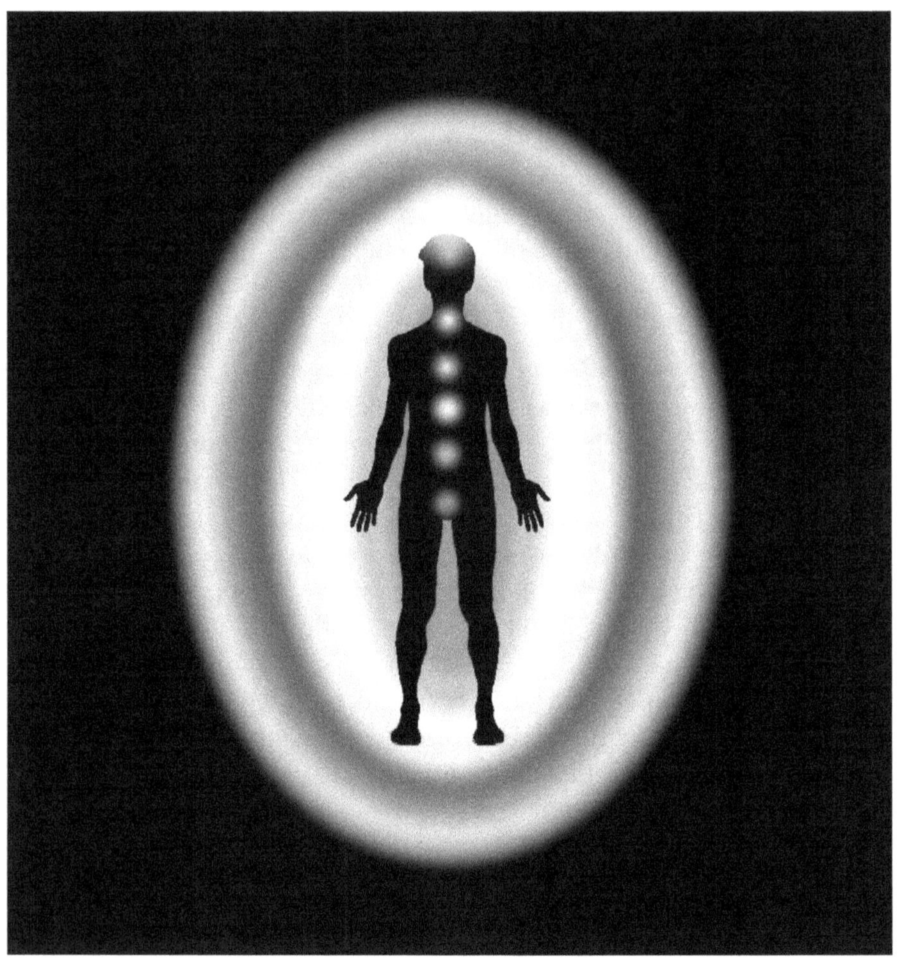

There are seven aura layers.[14]

Physical Layer

As the base layer of your aura, the physical layer sits on the surface of your skin, usually projecting up to a couple of inches from your body. This aura layer is connected to your root chakra and is closely related to all things physical. It is colloquially referred to as the physical layer because of its intimate connection to your physical body and state, but this layer is sometimes also referred to as the etheric layer. It's not to be confused with the fifth layer, which is often simplified as the "etheric layer," even though its full name is the etheric template layer or the etheric double body.

You can also see this layer as a bridge between your physical and energy bodies, responsible for conducting your spiritual energy to your physical body. There is a lot of interdependence between the physical layer of your aura and your physical state and health. This layer can also be affected by your thoughts and how you live your life, particularly regarding unhealthy habits and lifestyles. The more active you are, the stronger this auric layer will be.

Emotional Layer

As its name suggests, the emotional layer is connected with the things you feel on an emotional level. Adding another couple of inches on top of your physical layer, the emotional layer is associated with the sacral chakra, and its intensity can be altered by things like mood. All the positive or negative emotions you harbor will be reflected in this layer of your aura and can greatly intensify your aura as a whole.

The emotional layer is also considered to be the bridge between your mind and body, having the ability to influence your aura's physical layer and your body. Since emotions can be unpredictable and uncontrollable in a lot of people, your aura's emotional layer tends to be one of the most unstable layers, prone to sudden and rapid changes. The emotional layer's connection to the physical body through the first auric layer is the reason why chronic negative emotions and things like stress sometimes affect physical health. A well-known example of this interconnectedness is the way stress can diminish your immune system.

Mental Layer

The third layer reflects the solar plexus chakra and is indicative of your thoughts and beliefs. Mental clarity and stability are essential if this layer is to be kept healthy and strong. The mental layer is also responsible for attitudes, ways of thinking, discipline, ego, judgment, and much more. Naturally, this layer also reflects your intellect, logic, level of consciousness, and anything else that relates to your mind. Introspection, deep reflection, and intense thinking can expand this layer of your aura.

The mental layer isn't just about logic and your conscious thought processes, though. It's closely related to mental health as well and can reflect psychological problems. Since the human mind can get quite intense and your brain consumes so much energy, it's no surprise that the third layer usually vibrates at a higher frequency than the physical and emotional layers. Your mental layer is also stimulated by creativity and mental tasks.

Astral Layer

The fourth auric layer is the astral one, powered by the heart chakra and associated with a lot of the same aspects of the self. As in the descriptions of chakras, this central layer bridges the gap between the physical and spiritual aspects of your being. The last three layers, just like the last three chakras, are much more spiritual than physical, which makes them vibrate at higher frequencies. The astral layer enables the top and bottom three layers to communicate effectively.

You can consider these two groups as your physical and spiritual planes, and the astral layer is the conduit between these two different worlds of energy. This gives the fourth layer a crucial role in your spiritual development. The astral layer can be empowered through loving acts and deep connections with other people. Similarly, this layer tends to be weakened when romantic relationships, friendships, and familial bonds are broken.

Etheric Template Layer

Sometimes shortened to the etheric layer, the fifth of your auric layers accompanies the throat chakra. It's also known as the spiritual layer or the double body, although a lot of its associations are with your physical form. This layer is sometimes described as the spiritual blueprint of your physical body and, in some ways, mirrors the physical layer, which is why the two are often confused. In a way, it is a projection of your physical attributes on the spiritual plane.

This layer has a lot to do with all the things you externalize through speech, other forms of expression, creativity, and sound. Your etheric template is also tied to your identity in terms of personality and the kind of energy you project to the world. The etheric layer is empowered by clear expression, self-expression, and the speaking of truth. Because of its connection to sound, this layer also responds well to sound therapy.

Celestial Layer

Intertwined with your third eye chakra, the celestial layer becomes stronger as you develop your intuition. This layer is quite pronounced in people who have strong instincts and trust in their gut feeling when making decisions and taking action. Self-doubt and internal disconnect will diminish your celestial layer and make it difficult to form spiritual connections and reach for enlightenment.

The celestial layer also reflects wisdom and communicates with the subconscious part of your mind. It acts as a point of convergence for the spiritual and physical aspects of your mind, which is why this layer responds so well to meditation, yoga, and other exercises that seek to transcend the two realms. The celestial layer vibrates intensely and is sensitive to energies and communications that might be reaching you from beyond the visible realm. It's also associated with your capacity for unconditional love and responds to the same from external sources.

Causal Layer

The seventh and final layer goes by a few different names, such as the spiritual, absolute, and causal layer or the Ketheric template. By this layer, your aura can protrude a couple of feet from the surface of your skin or up to five feet if it's a powerful field. The causal layer is the most spiritual and abstract one, associated with a lot of things beyond simple human comprehension. It's connected to the soul, universal oneness, divinity, universal consciousness, and much more.

The causal layer relates to your crown chakra and vibrates at a frequency higher than all the other layers. Its energy is pronounced around individuals who have attained a higher level of spiritual development and are intimately connected to universal energy. Because it connects to the soul, one's place in the universal energy network, and one's path in this life, every person has a causal layer on their aura. However, this layer is strong and intense only around those who have made enough progress toward enlightenment. Intensifying your seventh auric layer requires advanced, persistent, deep meditation.

Other Aspects and Relation to Chakras

One way to interpret the connection between your aura and your chakras is to consider the aura as an embodiment of the chakra system as a whole. Each chakra contributes to a particular layer of the aura, adding different levels and attributes to your auric field. As they stack up on top of each other, the layers, reflecting your chakras, form one unified field of energy that surrounds your entire being, and not just in a physical sense. The spinning vortexes of energy located in your chakras paint one holistic picture of who you are as a physical and spiritual being.

Your aura can also change either through your efforts to change it or simply as a function of time. How your aura and overall energy will change is partly up to you, but it also depends on your natural development as a living organism. If you evolve as a person or introduce important changes into your life, your aura will respond and reflect the new you, just as it did in the past. Experiences and how you react to them emotionally and mentally can also affect your aura.

Another aspect that is particularly relevant for those with the talent to see auras is the *color*. As mentioned earlier, an aura will normally feature a range of different colors corresponding to its layers, which play a part in auric readings. Auric colors can also change based on mood, environment, or efforts at healing. Stressors like depression, general stress, illness, and other factors can make auric colors duller. There are different interpretations of this concept, but it's generally accepted that specific colors signify various aspects of the self:

- **Red** – Grounding, willpower, and high energy.
- **Orange** – Thoughtfulness, considerate attitude, and an adventurous spirit.
- **Yellow** – Amicability, tranquility, and creativity.
- **Green** – Sociability, care, and ease of communication.
- **Blue** – Spirituality, intuition, and independence of thought.
- **Indigo** – A curious mind, gentleness, and spiritual connection.
- **Violet** – Intelligence, wisdom, and an independent character.

Signs of a Weakened Aura

You don't have to be a seasoned spiritualist or psychic and see the aura with your own eyes to determine if there's something wrong with it. When imbalanced energies take hold, or the aura suffers from some other spiritual affliction, there will be many signs. When your aura is diminished, or under the effect of negative energy, this produces emotional, mental, spiritual, and sometimes even physical symptoms.

Physical Signs

On the physical level, a weak or imbalanced aura is associated with a range of specific ailments, but it's also accompanied by generalized physical debilitation. An overall lack of energy and fatigue are the most common physical manifestations of a weak aura. You might feel like you're never getting enough sleep or like every movement of your body exerts tremendous effort.

A sense of low energy or chronic pain can mean your aura is weak.[15]

You'll still be perfectly mobile, but your diminished energy will make you feel like you're lazy and in a constant stupor. Individuals with a strong aura are light on their feet and have no problem jumping into action. Their body feels energized and smooth in its movements, plentiful in strength and vitality. Chronic pain is another common sign of a struggling aura, especially when there are no clearly identifiable physical causes behind the problem.

Emotional Signs

A weak aura will make you feel emotionally drained and directionless, or it can make you easily overwhelmed by your troubles. When you're shielded by a healthy aura, you'll remain emotionally stable in the face of challenges and setbacks. When the aura is weak, you'll commonly feel all sorts of negative emotions and find it difficult to relate to others. On the flip side, an auric imbalance can make you too emotional, explosive, and dependent.

Irritability, mood swings, bouts of depression, and a lack of stimulation regardless of activities are some of the other common signs. It can also become difficult to form relationships or stay in touch with the people you care about, either because of your own emotional issues or the effects that your imbalanced aura has on others. You'll feel generally anxious, fearful, and on edge, mystified by your own emotions.

Mental Signs

The mentality of those with a weak aura tends to be negative, unassertive, low in self-esteem, and debilitating. You might develop a powerful negativity bias, which occurs when you forget how to notice the good in life and end up in a self-perpetuating cycle of looking for and finding all things negative. In such a state, it's difficult to find motivation and derive any joy from life.

Cognitive aspects like concentration and clarity of thought also accompany a diminished aura. You'll feel like your thoughts are racing in many directions with no semblance of control over your own thinking processes. You might start perceiving danger when there is none, lose all trust in people, and become overly critical and cynical.

Spiritual Signs

Spiritual signs of a weak aura often interact with emotional and mental issues. A weakened spirit will inevitably make you feel purposeless and hopeless, finding it difficult to see the value in the things you do. This can have devastating consequences for your overall motivation to get things done and improve yourself. A spiritual stupor is very noticeable in the higher layers of your aura, and it will eventually make you feel stuck.

Overall, the weakening of your aura can cause a profound and generalized feeling of disconnect. You might feel disconnected from your purpose, the universe, nature, divinity, and your own soul. You'll find it difficult to believe in anything higher, not just in terms of the divine but also life, human connections, and even morality.

External Clues

External clues that your aura is struggling include the ways in which you're affected by external factors and the impression you make on others. For instance, you might find it difficult to establish boundaries with other people, making you overly vulnerable and highly susceptible to the effects of negative energy. Negative energy can come spontaneously from other people or be deliberately directed at you, and a weakened aura will fail to stop it regardless.

You'll also have a sneaking suspicion that people react negatively to your presence or that you're somehow attracting negativity. This negativity goes beyond human interaction, including negative circumstances, bad situations, and general misfortune. Even if you're not really attracting bad luck, the aforementioned negativity bias might convince you that there is a pattern. In either case, an imbalance in your aura is the culprit.

Attempting to See the Aura

Seeing the aura around yourself or other people is considered an advanced skill that involves some psychic and clairvoyant abilities – or at least a lot of practice. Using a mirror, softening your gaze while squinting your eyes might enable you to see the contours of your aura around your whole body (or parts of it). The aura tends to be more noticeable around the head because of the higher frequency of the chakras around that area.

You might also try to experiment with your peripheral vision, as some people will find it easier to see the aura from that angle. Any colors or lights you notice could be indicative of your aura. All of the above applies to observing other people as well, and your particular talents may make it easier to see other people's aura than your own, or vice versa. Some of the descriptions by those who have developed the skill to see auras involve blurry white light that's fleeting when focused on, at least at first. Practice and the strength of the aura being observed will make the light more apparent or even colorful.

It's also worth noting that the observable aura is likely to project no more than a couple of inches from the body. Combined, the seven auric layers reach well beyond that length, but some layers are more visible than others. You can try to observe multiple people at the same time, especially in your peripheral vision. Take note of any subtle differences you might notice around these people, particularly in regard to the quality or quantity of light. Knowing more details about these people's moods and physical attributes can also be helpful.

To try observing your own aura at home, you should find a quiet, private place that features a white background, such as a plain white wall. You can also use a larger piece of paper if need be. Low light conditions are preferable because dimmer lights will cause less interference and make your aura's own lights more noticeable. You'll still need to see clearly, so don't make your environment completely dark.

As always, the first step is to enter a state of relaxation and commit your mind to the task. Sit down comfortably in a chair that supports your back and turn toward your bright background of choice. Raise one of your hands and turn the palm toward the white surface, keeping your fingers together for the moment. Focus on your hand and soften your gaze while squinting a bit, but don't strain your eyes too hard. Observe your hand intensely for about 30 seconds and try to notice any alterations of light or space around the outline of your hand.

Whether or not you see anything, stay focused on your hand and start slowly separating your fingers, shifting your visual focus to the space between the fingers. This is where you might start noticing a certain effect between the fingers, or if you had already seen it earlier, it might now intensify. With enough effort, you might start noticing an effect of altered light following the entire outline of your hand and fingers. If the light you notice at first seems dim, that doesn't necessarily mean your aura is weak. Most likely, it just means you need to practice your aura scanning more. This is a difficult exercise that demands firm focus and powerful visualization techniques, so you'll have to work on it a lot if you are to see any results at all as a beginner.

Chapter 4: Tools and Techniques for Easy Energy Healing

With the information you've learned about your energy, chakras, and aura, you now have a foundational understanding of the way your energy works, what centers it passes through, how it affects you, and how it's projected. Treading into the practical side, you can now begin delving into the actionable basics of energy healing, which are all about influencing your energy and making it work for your benefit.

This chapter will serve as a practical toolkit by introducing a whole variety of accessible tools and methods that will be applicable in various rituals and energy healing techniques. These tools will include things like crystal healing, smudging, aromatherapy, sound therapy, and other common techniques that are often found in energy work. These are the approaches used to balance chakras, cleanse auras, raise vibrations, and more. By learning what these techniques are, you'll be able to determine the best ways of applying them in your routines and rituals, especially those that you'll learn about in subsequent chapters.

An Introduction to Energy Healing Tools

Energy healing can be approached from many angles, leaving much room for adjustment and preference. When you learn about all the options available, you can create a tailored system that fits perfectly into your personal inclinations, schedule, lifestyle, and goals.

For some people, energy healing is a means of improving how they feel physically, while others might commit to energy work primarily as an exercise in spiritual growth. Your focus might also be on the emotional aspects of your life and health. You'll also be able to take a truly holistic approach that addresses all of these areas. The overview below will elaborate on a few common components found in various energy healing techniques.

Crystals and Chakras

The unique molecular structure and physical shape of certain crystals have long made them a staple in all sorts of energy work techniques and other spiritual rituals. Various crystals vibrate at specific frequencies that interact with your body's energy field in different ways. Crystals are often used for spiritual protection, energy cleansing, and a lot of different healing methods.

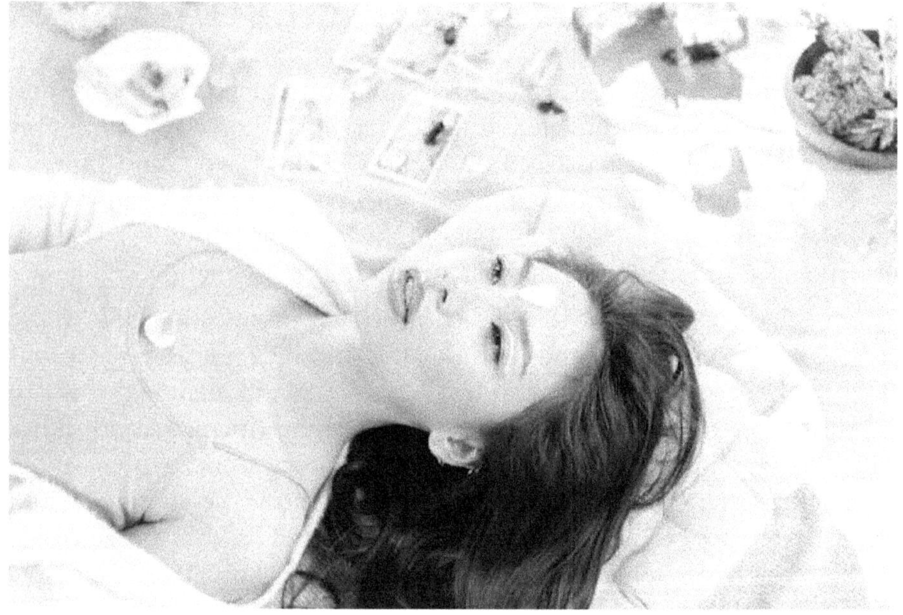

There are specific crystals that work in alignment with each chakra.[16]

Individual types of crystals interact particularly well with specific chakras, which is why a number of traditions assign these crystals as the go-to options for strengthening targeted chakras. In combination with chakra-specific chants, chakra-focused meditation, visualization, and colors, crystals provide a powerful additional layer of energy to stimulate your chakras. The chart below will outline the preferred crystals for each of your seven chakras:

- **Root Chakra** – Red jasper, hematite, black obsidian, black tourmaline, onyx
- **Sacral Chakra** – Carnelian, tiger eye, sunstone, orange calcite
- **Solar Plexus Chakra** – Pyrite, citrine, yellow calcite, amber
- **Heart Chakra** – Green aventurine, rose quartz, jade, rhodonite, amazonite, malachite
- **Throat Chakra** – Sodalite, celestite, lapis lazuli, aquamarine, blue kyanite
- **Third Eye Chakra** – Amethyst, moonstone, labradorite, purple fluorite
- **Crown Chakra** – Clear quartz, selenite, lepidolite, howlite

You can use your crystals in all sorts of ways that fit into your routine. A crystal can be carried on your person daily, incorporated into an altar, held during meditation, and much more. The important thing is to understand the crystal's energy and how it relates to your own energy and the healing process.

Crystals can be affected by external energies that can interfere with their energy fields, and they can also accumulate unwanted energy. On top of that, your crystals can also become weaker with repeated use. Luckily, cleansing and charging your crystals is a simple process in most cases.

The intention behind the ritual is the essential ingredient in cleansing and recharging a crystal. You can even cleanse your crystal under running water or in the rain if your intention is clear and strong enough. However, you should use Himalayan salt water or smudge your crystals with sacred herbs. Submerging a crystal in the solution with salt water will cleanse and charge it. Crystals can also be recharged in moonlight, sunlight, or by being buried under soil for 24 hours.

Crystals like selenite can also be used to clean other crystals or create your crystal charging station. If they're used intensely, your crystals will inevitably accumulate negative energies (in addition to becoming weaker), so cleansing and recharging are equally important. This is especially true for highly absorbent crystals like black tourmaline, which is known for its ability to soak up negative energy from locations where it's used for energy cleansing. Whatever methods of charging and cleansing you use, remember to set your intention before the ritual and make use of visualization.

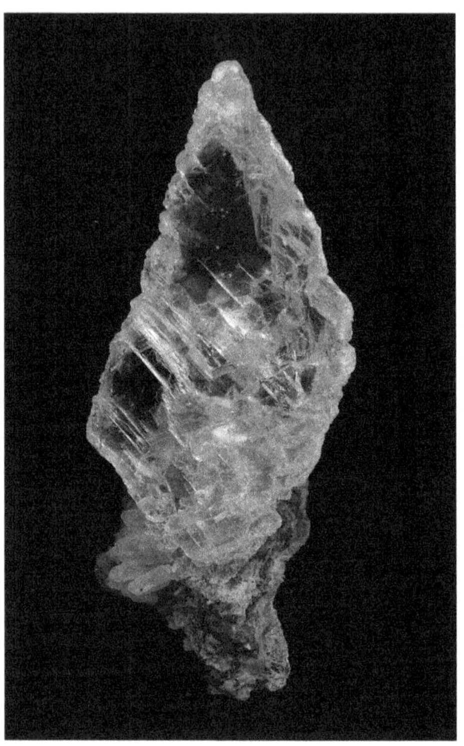

Selenite is a crystal that can be used to cleanse other crystals.[17]

Sound Vibrations and Your Energy

Various sound vibrations can have a range of potent effects on your energy. They will resonate with your energy centers like chakras and your aura as a whole, being able to break up blockages and restore balance. Sound is a powerful tool because it's a tangible, external source of energy that directly impacts your energy flow through physical action. That's why numerous forms of sound therapy and healing are being invented all the time and are becoming increasingly popular.

You'll soon learn that there are many ways for you to use external sounds to heal your energy, but you should also use the sounds that come from within you. Internal sound is especially relevant to chakra healing. As briefly mentioned in the earlier chakra overview, each chakra has a corresponding chant or mantra that resonates with its energy. This is because each chakra vibrates at a particular frequency, and they are activated by different sounds. A chakra chant is a simple sound that you'll make out of the depth of your vocal cords and maintain as long as your breath allows.

For basic chakra activation via sound or any ritual focusing on individual chakras, use the chart below as a quick reference:

- **Root Chakra** – Lam
- **Sacral Chakra** – Vam
- **Solar Plexus Chakra** – Ram
- **Heart Chakra** – Yam
- **Throat Chakra** – Ham
- **Third Eye Chakra** – Om
- **Crown Chakra** – Ah

Essential Oils

Essential oils are another widely applicable tool that's right at home in all sorts of energy-related exercises. Essential oils come from various sources and are used for an incredibly wide spectrum of goals. In short, they interact with the limbic system in your brain, which gives them a distinct ability to influence your emotional state and energy flow. In a broader sense, essential oils provide pleasant scents that can complement meditation, yoga, and other rituals. This is why they're often put into diffusers to enhance a desired ambiance.

Essential oils are another great tool to use to cleanse your energy.[18]

Essential oils are also commonly diluted and applied to specific parts of the body or used in showers and baths for greater energy cleansing. Your preferred essential oils can have positive effects on your aura, so they make a powerful ingredient in aura-cleansing sprays that can be used on the fly. These are frequently encountered in spiritual protection techniques, and they can be purchased or made at home.

In regard to chakras, you can apply diluted essential oils to any pulse points of energy on your body, especially in places where chakras are located. Different essential oils can target specific chakras (just like crystals, colors, and sounds), so it's important to know how they correspond. If you elect to incorporate essential oils into any rituals that will be discussed later, consult the correspondence summary below for targeted chakra healing:

- **Root Chakra** – Patchouli, myrrh, cedarwood, vetiver
- **Sacral Chakra** – Mandarin, rosewood, lemon, ylang-ylang
- **Solar Plexus Chakra** – Ginger, lavender, juniper berry, chamomile
- **Heart Chakra** – Geranium, maritime pine, rose, palmarosa
- **Throat Chakra** – Cypress, spearmint, frankincense, rosemary
- **Third Eye Chakra** – Clary sage, marjoram, sandalwood
- **Crown Chakra** – Peppermint, lotus, cedarwood, frankincense

Keep in mind that most of these essential oils will provide benefits for more than one chakra. You can use the above chart as a general guideline, but you are encouraged to experiment and find the combination most pleasant and energizing for you personally. Essential oils derived from lavender, lemon, and quite a few others will enhance chakra healing across the board, so you don't have to limit their use to just one chakra.

The Role of Colors

Colors play an important part in visualization exercises, but they also act as external factors in a similar way to sound. Colors are naturally stimulating to the human mind, which means they can affect the vibrations of your energy centers, your emotions, mood, and much more. There are many ways in which you can introduce colors as external stimuli in your rituals.

Colors are naturally stimulating to the human mind.[19]

Colored lights and candles are the simplest approaches, often used in meditation and various forms of energy work. As you'll soon learn, candles are a staple of spiritual practices in many different formats, but taking precautions against fire hazards is important. Visualization with colors also provides virtually limitless options for your energy-healing exercises. In subsequent rituals, refer to the list below as a quick reference point for the color correspondences of your chakras:

- **Root Chakra** – Red
- **Sacral Chakra** – Orange
- **Solar Plexus Chakra** – Yellow
- **Heart Chakra** – Green
- **Throat Chakra** – Blue
- **Third Eye Chakra** – Indigo
- **Crown Chakra** – Violet, white

Smudging Kits

Smudging is an essential cog in all manner of energy work, commonly used in specific rituals or to promote overall energy balance and positivity in your environment. Smudging can also be applied to objects and people for a more direct effect. If you are to engage in more complex energy healing techniques, you'd be well-advised to acquire a smudging kit.

Smudging kits can be purchased at affordable prices, but you can also put together your own kit. The latter can save you some money but also make your smudging kit more potent. This is because the care and intention you put into making your own smudging kit will infuse it with positive energy that you'll channel in the process. Setting the right intention is an essential aspect of many rituals and techniques in broader energy work, so a personal touch is often encouraged when you need certain tools.

Smudging is an old practice used for energy cleansing, notably among different native peoples in the Americas. It's usually done by burning a sage bundle in a certain space or around people and objects that are suspected of being affected by negative energies. By default, the preferred herb is white sage, but a whole range of other plants can also be used for a more tailored approach.

The best way to use smudging is to incorporate it into other rituals as a means of setting the right atmosphere and conditions that are more conducive to positive energies. Yoga, meditation, and simple relaxation can all benefit from smudging. As long as you take the necessary precautions when working with fire, you can use your smudge kit in whatever way you see fit.

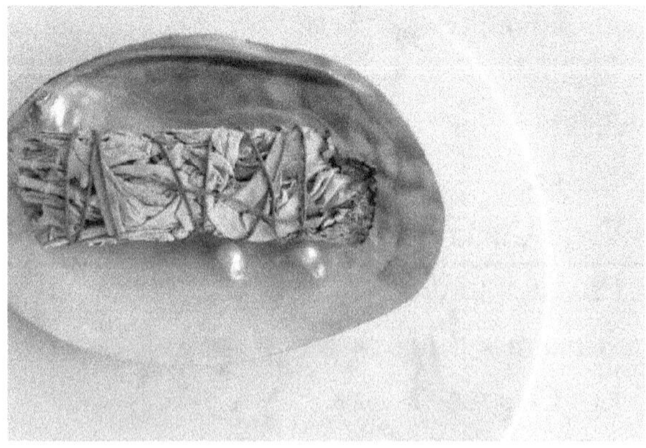

You can create your own smudging kit.[30]

A simple smudging kit consists of a stand or vessel, such as an abalone shell, which holds the plant being burned. A bundle of white sage, or other preferred plant, is then burned for about 20 seconds, blown out, and placed in the shell where it can safely smolder and spread the healing smoke. A typical kit consists of a vessel and a supply of at least a few prepared bundles.

Whether you're smudging or using herbs in some other way, your individual chakras will respond to specific herbs with preference, as with crystals. Refer to the breakdown below for guidance when picking ritual herbs to target your chakras:

- **Root Chakra** – Ginger, turmeric, ashwagandha
- **Sacral Chakra** – Shatavari, hibiscus, cinnamon
- **Solar Plexus Chakra** – Lemongrass, peppermint, chamomile
- **Heart Chakra** – Rose, moringa, neem
- **Throat Chakra** – Fennel, black pepper, pushkarmool
- **Third Eye Chakra** – Tulsi, shankhpushpi, cardamom
- **Crown Chakra** – Gotu kola, blue lotus, bacopa

Tools and Techniques in Practice

The next step is to apply the above tools and techniques in the most appropriate ways for your needs.

The following tools draw on the described principles to alter your energy in a way that promotes positivity and strengthens your energy body. These tools will inspire tranquility and have cleansing effects while enhancing any more complex rituals and routines you might engage in. Once you learn how they work in practice, you'll have an easier time incorporating these techniques into a personalized approach to energy healing.

Crystal Healing

With crystals, the first thing to do is get the right ones. A huge variety of crystals is available to purchase online, differing in terms of type, size, quality, and more. Consulting the chart outlined earlier, it's up to you to decide which crystals you need the most. The best option is to have at least one crystal for each chakra or at least cover those chakras that you feel are most in need.

Remember that crystal healing and the use of crystals in spiritual practices are broad topics. Crystals come in various forms, and they fulfill many purposes, from simple or elaborate rituals to being carried around as amulets. If you're building a dedicated space for meditation and other rituals, looking into crystals with a more generalized role is a good idea. Black tourmaline, for instance, is an excellent addition to any space because it absorbs negative energy.

Black tourmaline is great for absorbing negative energy.[21]

To conduct a simple crystal healing exercise focused on your chakras, pick your preferred crystal for each. Prepare your crystals, lie down in a quiet place, and make sure you are comfortable and free of distractions. Set a healing intention in your mind. Place an appropriate crystal on each chakra or just the chakras you're focusing on, close your eyes, and begin breathing gently and deeply. Focus on the crystals in your thoughts, fixating on the idea that they each possess their own unique energies and vibrations, which interact with the chakras.

Visualize the energy of the crystals by imagining it as a glowing light emanating from each crystal in its respective color. Turn your mind toward thoughts of healing, and visualize the crystals' energy growing stronger and brighter as it tunes into each chakra. Think of this process as a direct communication between your crystals and chakras, with each crystal's energy penetrating into the energy vortex and clearing any blockages.

Meditate on this process in your mind for at least ten to fifteen minutes, and once you're done, slowly remove the crystals in the order opposite to their initial placement. Once you're done meditating, round off the ritual by cleansing your crystals and letting them recharge through your preferred method. The more care and intention you put into each step, the more powerful the ritual will be.

Aromatherapy

Aromatherapy is one of the essential techniques in holistic healing practices. It relies on your sense of smell as a way of channeling energy into your body and promoting well-being on the physical, emotional, and spiritual levels. Essential oils are the key ingredient in this approach to healing because even a small concentration can fill up an entire space in a way that substantially affects all who are present.

Rely on the earlier chart to help you pick the essential oils that best resonate with the chakras you want to focus on and your goals. While many essential oils will positively affect all chakras, a targeted approach can often produce the strongest results. If you want to focus on more than one chakra, you can create an essential oil blend based on the chakras you need to align.

One way to get into basic aromatherapy is to use a diffuser to fill up your home or, ideally, your designated meditation room with the preferred scent. Just a few drops into a water-based diffuser can be more than enough, so it's best to start with small quantities and work your way up if necessary. With your diffuser doing its work, you can engage in your ritual of choice and use visualization to target a particular chakra. Simply sit or lie down comfortably, immerse yourself in the aroma, and focus on your chakras.

Invest in an aromatherapy diffuser to fill your home with the scents of your favorite essential oil.[22]

As the scent enters your nostrils, imagine it stimulating your chakra as it glows brighter. Breathe deeply and consistently, and spend as much time as you need in a state of calm. You can also use affirmations to further encourage an energy response to your meditative atmosphere. Verbalize your intention to release negativity and welcome in a new stream of positive energy, associating it with the scent of your favorite essential oil.

Sound Healing

If aromatherapy is a way for you to absorb healing energy via smell, then sound therapy is all about doing the same through your ears. There are many ways to go about this, ranging from simply listening to meditative sounds and music to elaborate rituals. You can create your own multi-layered, dedicated ritual that focuses on the use of sound. As an example, you might construct a three-layer ritual that uses background music, a singing bowl, and your own vocal cords.

Choose a preferred method of meditating on your chakras and find the ideal auditory background. You can play relaxing music, but you might prefer simple yet relaxing background noises, all of which are plentiful online. Prepare a singing bowl and retire to your meditative space. Assume the most comfortable position and start some basic meditation by slowing and deepening your breathing while meditating on your chakras. As an introduction, strike the singing bowl gently and allow the sound to resonate, fixating your thoughts on the sound as it propagates through the air and your body before dissipating.

Proceed by focusing on individual chakras one by one, starting at the root and slowly working your way up. Each time you visualize a chakra, start verbalizing its related chant and hit the bowl in a slightly different way to signify a change. Meditate on the cacophony of sounds and the physical sensations elicited by these many vibrations. Visualize the vibration as a stream of energy entering your chakra and clearing any blockage. Imagine your energy slowly becoming more balanced, your chakras aligned, and continue breathing deeply between the chants. Imagine yourself being bathed in sound waves throughout the whole ritual, considering it your sound bath. Spend as much time as you feel is appropriate until you feel balanced and aligned.

Color Visualization

As hinted earlier, candles are one of the best ways to potentiate your color visualization in chakra-focused meditation, as long as you're choosing safety and being careful. Your candles can be scented to improve the overall ambiance of your meditative space, but the really important factor is the color. Obtain colored candles that correspond to each chakra and arrange them in whatever form you find easiest to associate with your chakra system. Whether it's a straight line or a circle, make sure that they're arranged in the order of your chakras.

The aim of this color visualization exercise is to take a powerful external source of energy, such as a candle, and draw that energy toward clearing and aligning your chakras. The color of the candle acts as a common channel that brings an individual candle closer to a particular chakra. Once you've placed your candles in a quiet place for your meditation, sit or lie down and start relaxing by breathing deeply.

Begin by focusing on the red candle, visualizing it as a symbol of your root chakra. Light the candle and imagine yourself switching on a powerful node of energy that you will soon connect to your chakra for healing. This is a powerful intention that you should spend some time focusing on as the candle's flame reaches its strongest level. Visualize the light and heat as healing energy radiating into your body and reaching the chakra. Move on to the next candle and repeat the process until all seven are lit and synchronized with your chakras.

Visualize all of these colors entering your body in unison, just as your chakras are aligned and working together to ensure a free flow of energy. Together, these vortexes of energy translate into your aura, making your whole body more energized and protected. At this stage, you will have established an environment highly conducive to further meditation, so it's a good idea to spend some more time drifting away in your thoughts and engaging in various other visualization exercises focused on your chakras.

Aura Smudging

To smudge your aura, you would apply the same logic as with any other smudging. You simply have to burn a bundle of white sage and direct the healing smoke to yourself in whatever way feels right for you. You can put your smudging stand right next to you, wave a smoldering bundle around yourself by hand, or simply smudge your entire room. What matters is the intention behind the ritual and how you combine it with other practices.

Perhaps the best way to smudge your aura is to use a smudging kit as an additional layer of atmosphere while you're engaging in some of the other rituals discussed above. Choose your preferred herb and designate a special spot for your smudging stand, making sure it's a safe place with no fire hazards. Before any ritual, set the intention of absorbing the healing smoke directly into your aura or have it pass over your chakra areas. Visualize the smoke as a pleasant, healing cloud of energy that fills the room and interacts with your chakras, cleansing each one as it registers through your senses. You should also smudge any of the props you might be using, including crystals, candles, and other healing items.

Chapter 5: Healing Meditations and Breathwork

Since breathwork and meditation play such important roles in energy healing and your spiritual development, you'll find that they are foundational to an almost endless variety of spiritual exercises and energy work. This chapter will provide you with a deeper dive into breathwork and meditation, teaching you how you can use self-guided techniques to diversify your energy healing routines and create an approach that best suits your needs. It will feature details about different meditation styles, chakra-focused meditations, breathwork methods, different combinations, and more.

Meditation and Breathwork 101

As an entire body of spiritual techniques and traditions, meditation is a vast term with a long history behind it. Mindfulness, guided visualization, mantras, and many other techniques are only some of the components to consider. As a discipline, meditation is primarily mental in its methodology, leveraging intense awareness and the pursuit of inner peace to achieve desired results. The goals of a person's meditative routine can be a very broad spectrum, but the power of the mind and sharp mental focus is right at home in energy healing.

Meditation and breathwork will allow you to control your thoughts and harness the right kind of energy.[28]

Meditation owes its healing attributes to its ability to calm the mind and reduce stress, taking your consciousness to a place of tranquility and control. This inevitably reflects on your energy because it allows you to take the reins and direct the flow to where it's needed. In the case of energy healing, meditation is mostly used to clear the mind and enter a state of deep relaxation in which you can direct your energy to clear your chakras or heal and strengthen your aura.

With chakra-focused meditations, you'll be able to balance your energy centers like chakras. Chakra-focused meditation makes use of a number of previously discussed techniques as a way of targeting a specific chakra with as much intensity and focus as possible. Specific visualizations that rely on detailed descriptions of the chakras are one example. These visualizations seek to create powerful mental images of the chakra healing process, often conjuring up scenarios or going into outright internal journeying. Other chakra-specific tools, like chants or crystals, are always a welcome option to enhance such rituals.

Often accompanying meditation are the many techniques of breathwork. In yogic circles, breathwork or breath control is commonly referred to as pranayama and constitutes one of eight essential facets of classical yoga. Since breath and energy are often treated as one and the same in these traditions, pranayama can be interpreted as energy control.

Breathwork is sometimes used to prepare the practitioner for advanced meditation because it promotes mental clarity and tranquility, but it's still a very direct way of guiding your energy and has wide application in its own right. In either case, the connection between breathwork and meditation is substantial.

The role of breathing in techniques like basic mindfulness is usually more passive since breath is used as an object of focus and attention. This usually boils down to mere observation instead of trying to breathe a certain way. On the other hand, breathwork in practices like pranayama is a proactive approach that employs a whole range of different methods. Diaphragmatic, alternate nostril (Nadi Shodhana), and box breathing are only some examples. Some other techniques commonly found in pranayama include bellows breath (Bhastrika) and breath retention (Kumbhaka).

Breathing exercises such as these can have tremendous benefits on your mind and body beyond just calming you down. They can fundamentally reduce stress, help with emotional decompression, improve concentration, regulate your nervous system, soothe anxiety, improve sleep, and much more. These exercises will inevitably boost your energy flow and produce noticeable physical effects that you'll feel quite clearly. Overall, breathwork is essential in enhancing your body's self-healing process and encouraging your energy to flow freely and confidently to every corner of your being.

Combining meditative practices with breathwork will amplify the effects of both, but it's also important to remember the power of visualization. For instance, breath patterns in various breathwork exercises can be synced with intense visualizations and further enhanced by affirmations. Your breathwork will be the physical driver propelling your energy flow, while visualization helps direct your intention and essentially tells your energy where to go and why.

Similarly, affirmations can verbalize intentions and further intensify your efforts. An affirmation is a simple statement of intention or encouragement that can be woven into all sorts of rituals or basic daily routines. Affirmations are also a way to guide yourself through meditation by essentially giving yourself instructions on what you're visualizing and what goal you're pursuing. This can help you enter deep states of relaxation, release tension from your body, clear mental blocks, and more.

While beginner-level meditation and breathwork are simple in principle, a number of challenges might arise. You're likely to encounter some difficulties early on if you're the type of person who finds it difficult to relax. This is why it's important to leverage all of the techniques mentioned above and create combinations that work for you. Some folks can dive right into meditation through little more than basic mindfulness, but others might require diligent breathwork, intense visualization, and various props.

Many people will encounter Restlessness and difficulty focusing at some point in their energy work, and it can even happen to experienced practitioners. The only real way to break through these issues is to practice. It's best to start with simple exercises and to keep your meditations and breathwork mostly basic initially.

The same applies to the duration of your sessions, which shouldn't feel forced or like a chore. Keep it short and simple at first, practice regularly, and gradually bring your game up to higher levels. You should see focus as a skill that you can develop like any other, but it could require considerable time and effort. You can also make things easier on yourself by using gentle prompts and affirmations. The key is gradually easing into meditation and gently nudging your mind and body in that direction instead of diving deep and fast.

Exercises

With the options discussed in the above overview, you can move on to practical steps in your personal healing journey. You'll have considerable room for personalization in your energy healing routines, so it's up to your discretion how you'll combine and choose these techniques. As long as you observe the basic principles of energy work and consider your needs and circumstances, you can improvise and adapt as needed. The following exercises will provide instructions on several energy healing techniques you might consider.

Five-Minute Breathing Reset

With enough effort and practice, you can use short mindfulness rituals as a means of resetting your day, so to speak. When you're having a rough day or struggling with a hectic schedule, accumulating stress, hitting pause, and engaging in mindfulness for just five minutes can be just the thing to recharge your energy. This personal reset will allow you to take on the rest of the day more easily while also making you less vulnerable to negative energy in general.

You can do this almost completely on the fly because it only requires a five-minute break, which you can afford no matter how busy things get. A breathwork method that works particularly well with a five-minute reset is the 4-7-8 exercise. Inhale through your nose for four seconds, hold it in for seven, and exhale slowly and very gradually through your mouth for eight seconds.

As always, keep your focus on breathing to enter a state of mindfulness, and repeat this breathing pattern up to six times. Restore normal breathing if you have to for a few seconds, and then repeat the cycle again. Five minutes of this exercise will encourage your body to relax and release tension, both physically and mentally.

Chakra Alignment Practice

With enough focus and visualization, you might be able to activate and align your chakras solely through breathing. Recall what you've learned about chakra-focused meditation and the many associations used to symbolize each chakra in your mind. Combining this knowledge with the visualization of air as life energy, you'll be able to breathe and use your mind to direct that energy through your chakras in any way you see fit.

You can try creating a ten-minute chakra-focused meditation that relies solely on breathwork and visualization. Set your timer for ten minutes plus however long it takes you to relax before drifting off into meditation. Begin by lying down in bed comfortably and visualizing your chakras as you would during a chakra scan. Use your preferred breathing technique to relax and tune into the idea of air as energy entering your body.

Once you're fully focused, visualize the air you inhale as a stream of cleansing energy that enters through your heart chakra and pierces through to the next chakra. Going from top to bottom, spend some time on each chakra, visualizing it as a vortex of life energy with either a blockage or an attachment of negativity sapping its strength. The fresh, cleansing energy you draw with each breath will enter each chakra and act as a counterforce to the problem, opening up the chakra and restoring a balanced flow. If you feel that your chakras are extremely misaligned or blocked, it's a good idea to use an incremental approach, with each new session strengthening the chakra partially.

Grounding Breath Exercise

Grounding yourself through breathwork is all about deep breathing and visualization. Deep, diaphragmatic breaths will ensure that the air penetrates as deeply into your body as possible, making you feel physically engaged and present. Grounding always works best if you're in an environment that's conducive to feeling grounded, such as a natural outdoor setting. With some practice, however, a combination of visualization and concentrated breathing can help you become grounded almost anywhere.

Begin by breathing gently and deeply, taking breaths that are consistent and longer than usual but not too forcible. At first, focus solely on your breathing and the flow of energy through your lungs and into the rest of your body, imagining each breath as a wave that energizes and relaxes you. Once you've entered a state of relaxation, visualize roots growing through your legs and extending from your feet. The roots sprawl out around each foot, burrowing into the ground and providing a sense of stability while also feeding you natural energy that provides strength.

Cleansing Breath Meditation

Similar to chakra alignment breathwork, a simple cleansing breath meditation will begin with relaxation, focus, and a visualization of energy as traveling through air. This time, imagine the external life force as a white light being drawn to your crown chakra from above. This white light represents a benevolent force with powerful healing properties that pierces right through negative energy and dissipates it.

Inhale deeply and imagine this white light entering your chakra system from above. Visualize it entering your body, moving through the chakras, and spreading out beyond until it fills every part of your body. The light enters with every deep breath you inhale and seeks out any negative energy, wherever it might be hidden. As it makes contact with this negative energy, the white light wears it down, weakens it, and prepares it for expulsion.

As you exhale, imagine yourself releasing this processed negativity and ridding yourself of it forever. If you're feeling particularly afflicted by negative energy, you can take it slow and visualize each breath breaking off and expunging just a piece of that burden. Try to visualize the white light breaking the problem down into components, taking them out one at a time until you feel cleansed.

Heart-Centered Breathing

Centering on your heart chakra and that general area in your meditation and breathwork can be a valuable exercise in trying to alleviate stress or awaken compassion, not just for others but for the self as well. The way you breathe can have a considerable effect on your heart rate, so this exercise leverages both physical effects and visualization.

Any breathwork technique that relaxes you will work, but you can start by trying a simple five-second pattern at first. Breathing a bit slower and deeper than you're used to, smoothly inhale to a count of five and then exhale for another five. As you clear your mind and focus on controlling your breathing, gradually shift your attention to your heart area. Smooth, controlled breathing will slow your heart down and provide you with plenty of oxygen.

Visualize your heart becoming stronger and working gently and without tension. Continue your breathing pattern and keep visualizing how your heart is being energized along with your heart chakra. Pay attention to how the air and the energy it carries fill up your chest, and imagine this energy healing you both on a physical and emotional level.

Breath Retention – Kumbhaka

Breath retention, known in yogic circles as Kumbhaka Pranayama, emphasizes holding your breath after each inhale and exhale. In some practices, Kumbhaka is divided into two types, Antara and Bahya, respectively, which describe interior and outer breath retention. Some yoga practitioners opt for one of these at a time, which means that they'll be holding either after their inhale or their exhale only.

Assuming a meditative position with a straight posture, you can either place both your hands on your knees or keep them on your chest and abdomen to observe diaphragmatic breathing. Close your eyes and begin by breathing normally at first through the nose until you are relaxed and fully in control of your breathing. For internal retention, inhale deeply but smoothly for five seconds so that your lungs are filled to the brim. As you finish inhaling, lower your chin to your chest, close your nose with your fingers, and hold your breath while counting to five.

When you count to five, raise your head back up and release your nose, exhaling through your nose freely. The goal is to exhale gradually for double the time it took you to inhale and hold, which would be ten seconds in this case. This is known as a 1-1-2 breathing ratio. After considerable practice, you might be able to increase your counts but make sure that you maintain the same ratio. The above cycle should be repeated for about 10-15 minutes for a full Antara Kumbhaka session.

Alternate Nostril Breathing – Nadi Shodhana

Nadi Shodhana is a popular pranayama technique that relies on breathing through your nostrils in an alternating manner. As its original name implies when translated, the method works as a subtle energy-clearing technique of breathing. Alternate nostril breathing aims to calm your mind, release physical tension, reduce stress, and much more in the way of your overall well-being. It's commonly practiced in yoga and accompanied by yogic poses and other exercises, but it works very well on its own as well. As with other breathwork techniques that are somewhat intense, special precautions are advised for those with lung or heart problems.

Nadi Shodhana is the common alternate nostril breathing method, and it's done by inhaling through one nostril, holding your breath for two or three seconds, and then exhaling through the other nostril. There is also a variation of this exercise called Anulom Vilom, which is essentially the same, except that it foregoes holding one's breath upon inhalation. Alternate nostril breathing can be difficult for some people at first, but as you get more experience with Nadi Shodhana, you can try to prolong the time you spend holding your breath.

The exercise is fairly simple, emphasizing slow, continuous breathing and an intense focus on the breath itself. You can begin by meditating regularly, such as sitting down with your legs crossed. The important thing is to be comfortable and maintain good posture. Once positioned, place your left hand on your left knee and raise your right hand close to your nose.

Empty your lungs and then close your right nostril by pressing on it with your thumb. Inhale your next breath through the left nostril and close it with your index finger. This is where you can hold your breath for a couple of seconds. When you're ready to exhale, open your right nostril, exhale, inhale through the same nostril, and then close it again. Open your left nostril and exhale to close the cycle. Repeat this cycle for about five minutes or less if you're struggling for air, and make sure that you finish the exercise by exhaling through the left nostril.

5-4-3-2-1 Sensory Awareness

The so-called 5-4-3-2-1 technique is a simple yet highly effective mindfulness method that can act as a powerful grounding tool that you can use on the fly. It derives its somewhat peculiar name from the methodology behind the exercise. The technique consists of five main steps, which include naming five things you see, four things you touch (feel), three things you hear, two things you smell, and one thing you taste.

The allocation can be somewhat adjusted if you prefer to focus on four things you hear and three things you touch, for instance. Still, you generally want those senses that are the easiest to stimulate to have a higher number of focal points. In a given moment, it's much easier and more practical to find five things to see than five things to taste. The exercise aims to shift your focus to the present moment and your immediate surroundings to become grounded and mindful.

This technique is an easy way to get out of your head and let go of things like frustration, anxiety, and overall negativity. You can use the 5-4-3-2-1 sensory awareness method to prepare yourself for meditation, get your thoughts in order after waking up in the morning, or manage stress in difficult situations. You are encouraged to experiment with the structure of the technique if your circumstances demand it, but the important thing is to be able to ground yourself without much effort.

Breath Counting Meditation

Counting your breaths is probably one of the simplest meditative exercises there is. It's a very basic form of mindfulness that's all about observation instead of effort. The goal of this exercise is to fade out everything in your mind except your breathing and breath count. You can use whatever maximum number feels most comfortable, but ten is the general sweet spot.

Breath-counting meditation begins by drawing your attention to your breathing pattern, as with basic mindful breathing. Once you're fully aware of each breath, start to count them up to ten and then start over once you reach ten. Keep repeating this pattern on a loop until you begin feeling the calming effects. If you practice breath counting meditation frequently on a daily basis, it can have a positive effect on your overall focus in day-to-day tasks. It's about training the mind to commit to an object of focus and a task on command and stay there, which is why it trains to focus in the same way a targeted physical exercise strengthens a muscle group.

Doing the first couple of loops is easy enough, but you might be surprised by how difficult it can be to maintain focus for longer. A trained, disciplined mind will be able to continue counting the breaths despite external distractions and even in the face of stress. Over time, you'll gradually increase the duration of your focused breath counting and develop the ability to stay in your lane no matter the circumstances.

Box Breathing

Box breathing is a simple yet intense technique that alters the way you process oxygen, enabling you to relieve stress and anxiety or even lower your blood pressure and reduce pain. Because of its noticeable physical effects, it's best to first make sure that you don't suffer from a serious heart problem or another major health condition. The technique can certainly be practiced in those cases, too, but it's a good idea to consult your doctor about the specifics before getting into box breathing.

This technique is all about slow and deep breathing. Find a quiet place where you can sit upright in a chair, keeping your feet flat on the ground. Maintain a solid upright posture and place your hands in your lap, relaxing every muscle and leaving the palms facing upward. A straight posture and physical relaxation are important for allowing your lungs as much room as possible.

Begin by purging all oxygen from your lungs in a slow exhalation through the mouth while focusing all of your attention on this simple action. Then, take a deep breath through your nose, slowly counting to four as you inhale. As you inhale, engage your diaphragm and focus on the sensation of air filling your chest and then the abdomen. Hold your breath while counting slowly to four yet again, and then exhale through the mouth with the same count.

Make sure to physically sense a complete emptying of both your abdomen and chest as you exhale. Once emptied, hold your breath that way for another slow count of four before you inhale and repeat the process. Maintain this breathing pattern for as long as you feel comfortable, and remember to visualize the air as a powerful, healing force of energy.

Chapter 6: Visualizations and Journeys for Inner Peace

You've already seen how visualization plays an essential role in so many rituals and exercises aimed at energy healing. The reason for this is that energy work has so much to do with the mind and its innate power. External factors play their parts, too, but your mind ultimately has the power to influence your own energy and the way in which external energy affects you.

This chapter will focus more closely on visualization and how it works. You'll learn about the different ways in which visualization is used, and you'll also receive a rundown on a number of exercises to help you put what you've learned into practice. These techniques will revolve around guided visualization rituals and their power, as well as something called inner journeys.

Guided visualization methods are powerful tools for harnessing energy.[24]

The Role of Visualization and Adjacent Practices

In the simplest terms, visualization is the practice of manifesting your intention in the real world. Practically speaking, this means forming and focusing on a mental picture of a desired result so powerful that you make it a reality. Visualization is all about working with energies in the context of energy healing and many other spiritual practices. This means creating, molding, directing, and otherwise bending energy to your will. In energy healing, the goal is to use intentions and visualization to direct that energy toward healing, be it physical, emotional, or spiritual.

Visualization works directly with your energy body and can also tie into the subconscious mind. It allows you to correlate and articulate your intentions and inner nature clearly in your mind, doing so in a way that's difficult to verbalize. The significance of this is in the power of mental imagery, which allows every human mind to articulate its contents internally in a way that's much clearer than human language can explain. It's about all those things that make sense when examined in your thoughts, yet describing them with words proves difficult.

This is why the most powerful intentions are those that exist in your mind, which you can then meditate on. Visualization can allow you to tune into your energy in a way that few other exercises can. With enough practice, you'll be able to direct healing energy in whatever way you see fit, moving it to specific areas of the body. This includes chakra-focused meditation, but you can also target parts of your body in a physical sense. Visualization makes it possible to see the inner workings of your body, your chakras, energy flow, and aura so clearly that identifying and solving energy problems becomes much easier.

As you've seen in some of the earlier exercises, visualization can rely on things like colors and anything else that allows you to form unmistakable mental images. Chakras, for instance, are commonly visualized as vibrant, spinning wheels featuring certain colors. This universalizes the concept, brings it closer to human understanding, and allows for standardization across various traditions and schools of thought. Symbols are also often used in visualization because they can summarize and articulate broad, complex concepts. This is why symbolism plays such an important role in virtually all spiritual practices, both in mainline religions and esoteric circles.

Inner journeys are something else that this chapter will go into because of their association with visualization. A distinction should be made between the two, and the simplest way to summarize it is to say that inner journeying relies on visualization but goes much deeper. Basic visualization aimed at energy healing can be done on the fly, and visualization, in a broader sense, plays a role in everyone's daily life.

Journeying, on the other hand, entails deep meditation in controlled conditions, often relying on laborious meditation. It's also a way to dive deeper into your subconscious mind. Journeys often revolve around creating and visiting certain spaces in your mind, particularly those characterized by feelings of safety, peace, and understanding. Visualized journeys can also be about meeting people, entities, and spirits or interacting with universal energies at a more intimate level. For the purposes of energy healing, journeying is a way to process emotions, release tension, confront trauma, and much more.

Visualizations can and should become a part of your daily routine, starting with energy alignment exercises in the morning. These can include energetic centering, grounding, breathwork, and chakra alignment rituals that are combined with visualization. Daily affirmations can also enhance these routines, helping you set and verbalize your intentions as you begin a new day. This will reinforce your goals and remind you of the spiritual goals you want to achieve. Such routines can also be combined with quick mindfulness exercises to solidify your firm station in the present, making room for active gratitude for each present moment.

Visualization and Journeying Exercises

Using your ability to visualize scenarios and various forms of energy healing, you'll be able to enter deep states of relaxation, process emotions, and align yourself spiritually. This will inevitably lead to benefits for your physical health as well. The exercises outlined below will use visualization and inner journeying to harness your energy for healing and spiritual strengthening. They'll aim to do so by focusing on your chakras, aura, and overall energetic balance.

Inner Sanctuary Visualization

Visualizing an inner sanctuary is about creating a vivid and well-defined sacred space in your mind. By creating a powerful vision of this place, you can afford yourself a place of refuge where you can retreat in your moments of hardship and doubt. Acting as a sort of mental retreat where you can seek healing and clarity, this sanctuary can be a mental image of a house, an astral temple, or whatever else feels most comforting and secure to your sensibilities.

First, go to your usual meditation spot or any other location that evokes feelings of comfort, safety, and calm. It can also be an outside location, such as a tranquil garden or a natural area. Assume a comfortable, meditative position, lying or sitting down, and make sure there are no distractions around, particularly your phone and other devices. Start with a relaxing breathing exercise, close your eyes, and tune into the energy entering your system via breath. Observe this stream of healing energy as it passes through the airways and fills you up physically and spiritually. Release your stress and worries as you exhale, focusing only on the present moment and place, expelling all other concerns from your mind.

Find a tranquil place like a garden to visualize.[25]

The first place you'll visualize will be an abstract one, found somewhere deep in your mind that's beyond the reach of external interference. Meditate on the idea of withdrawing into this mental space and becoming untouchable. This is an exclusive place for which only you have the key. Gradually, begin painting a more defined picture of this place, imagining it as a home or temple. It's a remote but safe area that inspires a sense of healing and makes you feel welcome. Tell yourself internally that you can intuitively feel that the universe wanted you to arrive at this place in this very moment to give you a sanctuary where you can recuperate emotionally and spiritually.

Aura Bubble Visualization

You'll learn more about energy shielding in the next chapter, but the topic of visualization lends itself to a lot of exercises focused on making your aura stronger. This is usually done by projecting a mental shield around your aura, which aims to protect you and your aura from negativity. A common approach is to visualize an auric bubble, usually blue in color, which glows and casts a layer of protective light around your aura. This will make the aura more vibrant and resilient against negative energies and other unwanted external influences.

The blue bubble visualization begins in a similar way to other exercises that focus on visualizing energy in the form of light. Setting up an ambiance with real-world blue lights can greatly enhance the ritual. The significance of the color blue is in its association with balance, calm, wisdom, and wellness, in addition to the throat chakra. Through the association with wisdom, the color blue also relates to your mind, which matters because visualizing a shield is about casting a mental image into the real world. To visualize an auric bubble, subject yourself to a deep meditation exercise and establish a mental connection between blue light and energy.

Harness this blue light as you would a white light, internalizing and accumulating it around your throat chakra. Direct that energy to the outer-most layer of your aura and imagine it settling on top of your aura as a new, protective coat of energy. Imagine this layer of blue light expanding further and forming a bubble around your whole body, glowing brightly and protecting you. This exercise works best when you're feeling overwhelmed by stress and need to retreat for a few minutes of privacy and calm.

Healing Waterfall Journey

Waterfalls are a powerful symbol to incorporate into your visualizations and meditative journeys. Their water has a strong association with life, cleansing, refreshment, and the beauty of nature. Waterfalls can inspire a sense of tranquility, but at the same time, they also symbolize the power of nature. A waterfall is energy manifest, exhibiting power, flow, consistency, clarity, and many other concepts commonly found in energy healing.

Waterfalls are powerful symbols to incorporate into your visualizations.[26]

To use this potent metaphor in your visualization journey, visualize a special place not too different from your sanctuary. A healing waterfall can also be an element of your previously visualized sanctuary, such as a special corner of it dedicated to active healing. Start by visualizing a regular waterfall with as much detail and natural splendor as possible, including both its appearance and sound. You might also want to play a long background sound of a waterfall to potentiate this meditation.

Focus on the mental image of this waterfall flowing with determination and powerful energy yet also with a kind of welcoming gentleness. It's a large and mighty waterfall, but it doesn't flow too forcefully. Imagine the water particles sparkling as they diffuse in the air around the waterfall as an ethereal mist. Focus on the sparkles, gradually shifting to the idea that this waterfall is made up of pure light energy.

The waterfall glows white and elicits feelings of healing and wellness that you find welcoming. Imagine yourself as a consciousness journeying closer to the waterfall, eager to absorb its healing power. As you get closer, visualize your body entering this welcoming stream of light and healing liquid, standing directly under it. As the light envelops your body, breathe deeply to inhale its energy and release stress and negativity as you exhale. The sensation of the waterfall and its light on your skin is profoundly refreshing and rejuvenating.

Rainbow Chakra Journey

If you so choose, a rainbow chakra visualization journey can be an excellent exercise to attach to the visualization discussed above. The mist that floats around a waterfall can often produce a rainbow if sunlight hits it at the right angle, which is why rainbows are often associated with waterfalls. Visualize a bright rainbow forming next to your healing waterfall, showing the colors related to the seven chakras.

You can connect the rainbow to the waterfall visual.[27]

Visualize the rainbow toward the end of your healing waterfall visualization and meditate on the symbolism of this rainbow representing the chakra system. Gradually shift your mental gears toward focusing exclusively on your chakras and their respective colors. Imagine yourself as a consciousness floating toward the rainbow, now fully representing your chakras, and immerse yourself in the colorful light.

Visualize journeying through your own chakras in first person, starting at the root chakra and passing through the rest in the proper order. As you pass through the chakras, you are carrying the light of the rainbow in each of the chakra colors, filling every chakra with the right color and energizing it. Imagine each chakra growing brighter in its respective color as your spiritual presence feeds the light into it. Journey through the chakras as a healer, carrying your intention as you go along. When you're ready, exit through the crown chakra and return to your sanctuary.

Sacred Space Creation

Visualizing your personal sacred space will work very similarly to imagining an inner sanctuary. The main difference is in its sacredness dimension, which means that this mental space is sacred to you. It can be sacred because of religious undertones or special personal meaning, but the important thing is that this space is truly yours and speaks to you on a deeply spiritual level that's hard to describe to other people.

If you want to visualize this sacred space through your mainline religion, you'll find a lot of inspiration in your scripture and traditions. On the other hand, visualizing a sacred space that relates to you as an individual is a highly personalized exercise where you will paint a special mental picture that you understand in a way that few other people could. To visualize this space, you should spend some time in a combination of deep meditation and breathwork until the outside world fades away as much as possible. Make yourself completely comfortable, keep the lights dim or off, and close your eyes.

Imagine a journey through your mind's eye, picturing this as the most remote recess of your consciousness, a place that you must journey to. You can visualize the eye of your mind as a distant planet covered by an atmosphere with a thick layer of clouds. Visualize the existence of a special place of spiritual healing somewhere on the surface, beneath these clouds. Imagine your consciousness approaching this planet and start to visualize your sacred space. As you add more details to the mental image of this space, imagine the clouds slowly dissipating as you descend. When you have a clear image of your sacred space, you can come down and enter it. Focus on how this special place makes you feel, and prolong your stay by visualizing more details and scenarios.

Golden Cord Grounding Exercise

In basic grounding exercises, you can visualize roots growing out of your feet, as discussed earlier, but it's really a matter of personal preference. You can ground yourself via any number of mental images, with another popular one being the golden cord method. To start, come to a state of relaxation, presence, and focus, as discussed earlier, arriving at the point where you'd otherwise visualize the roots connecting you to the ground.

This time, visualize a golden cord that reaches down from the universe, feeding vital energy into your crown chakra and extending through the rest of your chakra system. The golden cord then exits through your root chakra and reaches down into the earth, going all the way to the earth's core and plugging right into its massive pool of energy. The cord feeds back and forth, infusing your body and mind with powerful energy – as well as stability, strength, and resilience.

The golden cord grounds you firmly and encourages mindfulness and tranquility in everything you do. Imagine it as your own private line of communication that inseparably connects you to a network of energy shared by the earth below and the heavens above. Visualize yourself as a small but essential node in this energy system, serving as a transfer point between the Earth and the universe.

Light Infusion Practice

Light infusion is a simple visualization exercise that works with energy imagined in the form of light. A way to enhance this exercise would be to use external light sources to make visualization easier and more vivid. For instance, you can use this exercise to strengthen your chakras and infuse light into them with the power of your mind. To do this, retire to your meditation space and set up seven colored candles corresponding to each of the chakras.

Arrange the candles in a way that allows you to see all of them and place them in the correct chakra order. Light them and begin with some basic meditation, mindfulness, and preferred breathwork techniques until you're ready to visualize. The objective of this exercise is to inhale healing light and pass it on to a chakra. Begin by visualizing energy as light coming from a candle and traveling through the air, entering your body as you inhale.

Start with the red candle for your root chakra, inhale the light, close your eyes, and direct that energy to your chakra with the intention of healing it and removing blockages. Repeat the process for each of the chakras and their respective candles, spending as much time as you feel is appropriate on each chakra. When you're satisfied that you've addressed all the chakras, finish the exercise by trying to focus on all of the candles at once. Visualize their light, combining into one intense stream of energy that you can inhale. Imagine this healing light filling your entire body and aura with warmth and vitality, settling in the outer layers of the aura.

Energy Field Expansion

Energy field or body expansion is a technique you can use to encourage energy balance and strengthen your aura. It can also be referred to as an aura expansion visualization. This visualization works best if you've developed the techniques of seeing or at least sensing the aura, as your ability to perceive the aura's presence will greatly enhance your ability to directly influence its power.

A simple way to do this is via a modified white light visualization, in which you'll use white light to feed your aura instead of pulling it through your chakras. Recall how you would pull white light into your chakras and then direct it so that it passes through your chakras gradually and clears blockages. To expand your aura, you can also begin by visualizing a white light of healing energy above your head and pulling it into your body. Breathe the light in or bring it down through your crown chakra, but keep your aura in mind.

Set the intention of using this white light to expand your aura as you draw in the energy. When you've fully absorbed the light and allowed it to spread throughout your body, you can begin using it directly on your aura. Simply visualize accumulating this energy in the center of your body, ideally around the heart chakra, and use your thoughts to direct it outward in all directions, with an even amount of energy in each direction. The idea is for this light energy to push the aura outward and expand it as it exits. You can use your exhales as a physical association to enhance this visualization. As you exhale, imagine the energy pressing outward, and when you inhale, associate the expansion of your chest and abdomen with the expansion of your overall energy field.

Chapter 7: Shielding Your Energy from Negativity

Shielding your energy and combating negativity is a spiritual discipline in its own right, but it also ties into energy healing. Energy shielding and cleansing are usually categorized under spiritual protection, and its elements include certain practices that are right at home in healing. After all, good health relies on prevention just as much as treatment.

It's important to learn how to shield your energy from negativity.[28]

When it comes to combating negative energy, there are times for energy clearing and times for building up your defenses. This chapter will delve into some basic precepts of spiritual protection and teach you how you can defend your energy from unwelcome external influences. You'll learn more about what negative energy is and how it can be countered before diving into a few practical exercises that will shore up your defenses.

Spiritual and Energy Protection 101

The first step toward shielding your energy is to understand what you're up against. Negative energy is a term that's thrown around a lot and used in all sorts of contexts, giving it a variety of meanings. With respect to energy work and healing, negative energy can be defined as an accumulation of unwanted energies or vibrations that interfere with your normal energy flow. Such energy can build up in your chakras and cause blockages or attach to your aura and weaken it, and it can come from many sources.

Some negative energy is spontaneous, but it tends to emerge as a consequence of ill intentions, trauma, certain behaviors, and unresolved emotional and spiritual problems. People are perhaps the most common conduits of such negativity, and they can produce and direct it at other people with intent or spontaneously. This means that a lot of the negativity you'll encounter comes from others but can also come from within you. Negative energy can also linger in spaces or around objects as a residue left behind by the presence of negative people or events.

Understanding and detecting negative energy has a lot to do with your intuition. Everyone has the innate ability to sense negativity, with some people's senses being sharper than those of others. When you get that inexplicable yet familiar feeling that a person just rubs you wrong or a place doesn't feel right for some reason, you are intuitively sensing negative energy. Intuition is a powerful tool that can get rusty if it's not used regularly, but it tends to respond to negative energy with a particular intensity.

Negative energy can also be a less clearly defined yet perpetual feeling that somehow permeates your entire life. When you feel that nothing ever goes right for you or that you attract bad luck, it's often a sign that negative energy lingers around you. Negativity can infiltrate into every crevice of your life and inflict tremendous damage on your mental health, relationships, motivation, and much more. When the signs of a negative energy buildup are ignored, the problem is very unlikely to resolve itself spontaneously. More often, negativity will fester and grow until it overwhelms you. Frequent contact with such energies will lead to anxiety, fatigue, lethargy, irritability, sleep disruption, and various other problems.

Energy healing can do the trick when you're facing negativity that comes from within you or unwanted energy from an unknown source that seems to follow you around. When it comes from other people, however, you'll need to defend yourself, not just heal. This is especially true if you're dealing with toxic environments on a daily basis, be it at home, at work, or anywhere else. Badmouthing, gossiping, scheming, and overall interpersonal friction are channels of negative energy that are all too common. When such an environment takes hold at work, physically avoiding these influences can be very difficult. That's where energy shielding and spiritual protection come into play.

Unintentional negative energy from other people comes as a consequence of these people's own problems and imbalances. They struggle spiritually or emotionally, and this simply rubs off on other people sometimes. They don't mean to hurt you, but their influence is an energetic contaminant that can creep its way into your own energy body if you don't know what you're dealing with. On the other hand, there are malicious actors who understand the concept of energy very well and use it for nefarious purposes.

Such individuals will use psychic channels and even elaborate rituals to target someone else's energy with negative intentions. There are also those who don't partake in spiritual practices but simply feed on negativity, hurling it at others through speech and behavior. They might also use subtle yet powerful forms of human communication, such as empathy, to deliberately channel negativity at you.

The best way to detect negative energy is to look for the aforementioned signs and symptoms, combining them with your intuition and instinct. If negative energy has accumulated in your energy body or chakras, you will inevitably feel emotional drain, exhaustion, frustration, anxiety, and all those other symptoms that clearly show that something is amiss with your energy. You can also observe how you interact with others and how you make them feel. Having difficulty relating to others or having constructive conversations with them is a common sign that you harbor negative energy. It will also interfere with your empathy, making you judgmental, overly critical, restless, and impatient.

Many of the exercises already discussed in this book will help you clear negativity, but to prevent it, you have to shield your energy. Energy shielding is done by creating energetic boundaries, which function as invisible buffers between you and unwanted external energies. You can establish these shields through various rituals, a number of which revolve around visualization. Typical shielding visualizations include energy bubbles, mirrors, expansions, and similar exercises aimed at fortifying your energy.

Meditation, self-awareness, and mindfulness can also contribute to energetic protection. Sometimes, the best form of energy shielding relies on a personalized approach that's empowered by intentions and goals that are unique to your needs. Meditating on things that you associate most closely with protection, security, and resilience for personal reasons will enhance any exercise. You can also rely on physical props that are known for their protective qualities, such as salt, crystals, and other tools.

Shielding in Practice

These exercises and tools will employ a combination of visualization, breathwork, spiritual props, and some mental adjustment. Their goal is to tackle negative energy directly and stop it in its tracks or at least strengthen the layers of protection against your energy body to weaken the effects of negativity. Remember that no spiritual practice has to exist in isolation, so it's always a good idea to integrate the knowledge you've gained in previous chapters wherever it's applicable.

Light Bubble Shield

Drawing on what you've learned about aura bubbles in the previous chapter, you can further modify this visualization to create a more generalized bubble-shaped shield around yourself. The way your energy bubble protects you is all about the intention you set. Whereas the aura bubble discussed previously relied on the color blue and its powerful associations, your generalized bubble shield can be built upon white or golden light.

These colors can be associated with divinity, so you can visualize your light bubble shield as a form of personal protection descending from above just to protect you. This protective light that settles around your body comes in the form of light, but it's absorbed and spread out through your breathing. Imagine it as a containment shield that needs fuel to run, with that fuel being the air you breathe. With each breath, the light bubble grows stronger and shines brighter.

You can also visualize a smaller bubble in your abdomen, functioning as a miniature version that acts as a processor running the shield. Place your hand on your abdomen, and make sure that you engage your diaphragm as you breathe in and out. Feel it expanding and contracting as it feeds air and energy into the light bubble around your body.

Visualize how negativity and all the other unwanted external influences are hitting the outer layers of the bubble and being broken down into bits of disparate negative energy that dissipate into the air around you. Use an affirmation to reinforce the point and remind yourself that you're being actively protected from whatever interference you're trying to avoid at the moment.

Reflective Mirror Shield

If you visualize energy as light, you can apply the same principle to negative energies. This means that you can visualize an energy shield in the form of a mirror that fully deflects external energy and keeps you protected. Visualizing this mirror shield with care is necessary because you don't want to reflect positive or healing energy as well. It can take quite a bit of effort to visualize a selective energy shield, so make sure that you can afford the time for deeper meditation.

There might also be instances where you can afford to reflect all energy because yours is well-balanced and aligned. For example, you might find yourself in a situation where you'll be exposed to negativity for a very brief period. In those cases, you can set aside a few minutes for some basic mindfulness and start visualizing a simple mirror shield that keeps you completely isolated from all external influences.

Imagine it as a shield you'll soon turn off when you leave the current situation and physically remove yourself from the negativity. Once you're in the clear, the shield can come down, and you can begin opening yourself up to outside energy and resume your role in the larger system of universal energy. It's a way to disconnect briefly in emergency situations when you don't have the time to visualize too deeply and can't leave right away.

Grounding Cord

As you've probably realized by now, grounding can be done through a practically limitless variety of visualizations and other techniques. You should always strive to use the visualization that resonates with you the most and makes sense in your mind. Visualizing roots extending from your feet into the ground is a popular approach, but it might not be the best choice as a form of energy shielding. Energy shielding is usually something you want to maintain on the move, and it can be difficult to visualize yourself growing roots and moving at the same time. In fact, being fixed in place is one of the first associations with roots.

To shield yourself via grounding is to draw a continuous stream of rejuvenating energy from the earth, using it to provide a sense of constant stability that makes you and your energy less vulnerable. One way to visualize this is by imagining an invisible cord of energy that functions as your anchor to the earth below. When you feel like you're being thrown off balance, take a few minutes to relax through some breathwork and start the exercise like any other grounding technique.

Imagine a cord that passes through your chakras from top to bottom, branching out from one or more of the chakras and reaching into the ground. Picture how this cord feeds into your chakra system as a communication cable, sending energy back and forth and drawing stability from the ground. Visualize this cord also sending any accumulated negativity into the ground, where it dissipates into the vastness of the earth. Most importantly, consider this cord an elastic string that can stay attached to your anchor point no matter where you go.

Affirmation Shielding

As always, affirmations might come in handy if you need to enhance any or all of your other shielding techniques. Affirmation shielding simply means using specific affirmations that relate to the idea of energy shielding and spiritual protection. They can be anything that you can easily associate with these concepts, including words of simple encouragement or statements referring explicitly to energy shielding.

Create a series of affirmations that reinforce the thought that you are protected and safe, thanks to the balance and harmony of your energy. You can also make your affirmations refer to your place in the wider life energy of the universe, which flows through and energizes all things in existence. Putting your energy into the context of a larger, all-powerful system of energy will give you an empowered perspective and courage.

When you feel that you are truly in tune with vital energy, it's going to be difficult to imagine something as small as a burst of negative energy from a toxic individual knocking you off balance. This will provide a layer of mental shielding that will undoubtedly translate into a more resistant energy field around you. Make your affirmations exude confidence and use them as reminders of all your valuable work with energy healing. Maintain the awareness that you're employing a wide arsenal of techniques and rituals that have made your energy stronger and more stable.

Breathwork for Shielding

Breathwork, or breathing in a broader sense, can play three distinct roles in energy shielding. As with any energy exercise, its first role is to induce relaxation and help you transition into a meditative state. Secondly, breathing helps you visualize the entry of healing energy into your body, which you'll then use in accordance with your ritual. Thirdly, visualizations that revolve around creating or expanding energy fields and shields around you can use the expansion of your body during inhalation to enhance the mental images that you need for the exercise.

You can also create a simplistic energy shielding technique that relies primarily on breathwork. All you have to do is engage in a breathwork exercise and visualize yourself pulling in energy as you would in other rituals. However, focus on the idea that the energy you're inhaling is protective instead of just healing. Imagine this energy seeping into every corner of your body and making you more resilient. Then, use the action of your lungs and abdomen to accumulate and expand your protective energy shield.

You can modify this exercise and experiment with it however you see fit. For example, you might want to visualize a protective energy that spreads out across your body and concentrates in multiple locations that house your chakras. Because your aura is external, most energy shielding exercises focus on protecting it instead of the internal aspects of your energy, like chakras. This doesn't mean that chakras don't need shielding, however. Since some negativity can come from within, shielding your chakras shouldn't be neglected.

Salt and Water Rituals

Salt is a potent tool in all manner of spiritual protection techniques, and it can be used for both cleansing and protection. When it comes to cleansing negativity from your energy, salt is usually combined with water in things like salt water baths. For all purposes, you generally want to use specific types of salt like Himalayan pink or Epsom. A saltwater bath once a week will do wonders for suppressing negative energy and improving your energy flow. Epsom salt has the added benefits of subduing or preventing inflammation, relieving pain, and a number of other effects on your physical health.

Salt is a potent spiritual tool.[39]

Another protective combination between salt and water is found in aura shielding sprays. Simply make your mix and pour it into a spray bottle that you can carry and use on the fly. To spray your aura with protective liquids, you'll be spraying the solution around yourself, not necessarily onto your skin. The effect of such a spray is that it enhances your energy field and encourages its vibrancy and expansion.

Since salt acts as a repellant against negativity, you can use it to keep negative energy away instead of cleansing it after the fact. Strategically placing small amounts of your preferred salt around your home is a way to establish energetic boundaries and keep negativity away. This approach is often used in unison with crystals placed around the home or other important spaces. Small vials of salt water can work in a similar fashion with respect to your body. They are practical and easy to carry, and they have the additional convenience of allowing you to use the protective liquid as you see fit.

Thought Management

The way you think is one of the most decisive factors in how vulnerable or resistant you are to negativity or any other energetic influence you want to avoid. Negative thoughts are an endless, internal source of negative energy that you'll carry around with you like a malign amulet sapping your strength throughout your day. Learning how to free yourself of these thoughts or reframe them into empowering ones is an essential exercise in energy healing and spirituality in general.

Whenever you have a negative thought, try to stop for a moment and analyze it. Look for ways in which these thoughts can be flipped around and turned into something positive, constructive, and empowering. For instance, if you suffer a major setback or any kind of failure, your default impulse might be to dwell on its negative consequences and beat yourself down with self-deprecating thoughts.

Instead, try to think of each failure as a lesson that you can use to achieve better outcomes in the future. When you see setbacks as learning opportunities instead of as signs of personal inadequacy or reasons to quit, you will be able to take every rough patch in stride. The first step toward that mentality is to acknowledge that everyone experiences failures and that they are a universal part of the human experience. Apply this same approach to any other sources of negative thinking in your life. Stop, deconstruct, and look for gain. It's a simple formula that happens to work wonders if you make an effort to practice it. This isn't about blind optimism either, as highlighting the universality of failure and the lessons it carries is merely a statement of fact.

Encourage yourself toward positive frames of mind through affirmations that highlight your qualities and values as an individual. Remind yourself that you are out in the world to attract positivity and pursue enlightenment, not to get hung up on negative thought loops and keep yourself stagnant. Meditate on the good things in life and make an earnest effort to always find the silver lining.

Chapter 8: Daily Energy Practices for a Fulfilling Life

This final chapter will bring an important point home, which is that energy healing isn't a one-time permanent fix to spiritual problems. It is not a pill that you can take for a month and then go right back to your old ways and never succumb to energetic weakness again. With people who are going through a rough patch but live an otherwise fulfilling life, it might work that way to an extent. For most purposes, however, energy healing and energy work, in general, should be seen as a lifestyle.

Daily practices will bring you closer to leading a fulfilling life.[80]

Energy Work as a Way of Life

Indeed, your energy healing journey is a set of practices and principles that you should incorporate into everyday routines. This is the best way to make these rituals truly shine and produce the most benefit, leading to a more balanced and fulfilling life. Now that you understand what your energy is and how it plays a part in a larger system, you should internalize that discovery and infuse it into your worldview and outlook on life. Starting with an understanding that a common vital force connects all things in the universe, you should form habits and ways of thinking that foster that interconnectedness and positivity.

These are simple habits backed up by powerful intentions that are meant to promote physical, emotional, and spiritual well-being. Energy healing should, therefore, be intentional, mindful, and consistent. It should consist of adopting a certain mentality just as much as exercises and rituals. Once you've harmonized your energy and boosted your vitality through all of these exercises, engaging in energy maintenance ensures you can make your newfound peaceful state of mind a persistent reality.

To make energy healing part of your daily life, you won't have to meditate for hours every day and make your every waking moment a spiritual endeavor. You simply have to be mindful and at least briefly check in with the energies that affect you every day. Brief morning alignments, simple morning breathwork, daily affirmations, and mindfulness in routine daily tasks are all equally valid strategies.

Regular energy work is the best way to create a stable, energetic foundation, not just because it directly affects your energy but also because of the way it reinforces your mentality. It makes energy healing into something you rely on daily, turning it into a staple of your overall wellness. After enough practice, you'll get to a point where your mind will create an inseparable association between energy work and feeling better. Once this happens, your faith in the journey and your familiarity with the concepts will make every intention much more powerful. Each ritual will thus channel more energy and provide greater returns on the time you invest.

Another thing about routines is that they provide structure and regularity by acting as anchors for emotional and physical balance. This encourages a steady flow of energy throughout your day and keeps you on track. Regularity makes your mind accustomed to this steady flow of energy, reinforcing energy pathways and making them stronger over time. This happens in the same way that physical exercise strengthens your muscles. Paths frequently traveled are the clearest in the physical and spiritual realms alike.

All of these contributing factors will eventually make energy work second nature for you. After a certain interval, you will no longer have to think too hard or spend a lot of time planning your energy-healing routines. You will simply do them because they're part of your daily reality, just like a million other things you do every day to sustain yourself. Getting out of bed will become a signal for introspection and for shifting your thoughts to the way your energy flows through you.

Morning routines are especially important for energetic balance because they set the tone for the rest of your day. If you make sure that your energy is aligned soon after waking up, clarity, purpose, and emotional resilience will follow you wherever you go. This applies to a lot of the exercises and rituals you've learned in this book. If you can choose the time of day for these exercises, mornings are usually the best choice. Since some rituals take more time and effort, it might not always be practical to carry them out before work, which makes them excellent for starting your weekend.

The way you end your day also matters, of course, and some rituals are undoubtedly more appropriate for when you're feeling like your energy has been sapped by a long and hard day. This will ensure that you sleep better and wake up feeling more energized than you would if you just collapsed on your bed the moment you came home in the evening. How much you want to rely on your mornings or evenings is up to you, but if possible, you should always have your day begin and end with at least some basic energy work.

Overall, consistent energy maintenance is the name of the game. Energy maintenance will promote a consistent flow of energy that prevents energetic stagnation or the accumulation of negativity. You need to regularly rejuvenate your energy and ensure it's flowing in and out every day. Feeling energized and balanced is not a sign that you should stop for a while. On the contrary, it means that you've achieved great results through your energy healing routine and should now focus on preserving those results in the long term. Consistent mindful actions and self-care will sustain vitality and encourage emotional clarity.

Practical Daily Routines

The following daily routines are simple exercises that will act as your energetic foundation and complement your primary energy healing rituals that you'll probably be doing with less frequency. They combine basic visualizations, affirmations, quick breathwork, mindfulness, and practical rituals meant to reinforce your new perspective on energy. Their simplicity is what allows these routines to become a part of your daily life, but if your circumstances allow, you should feel free to prolong them and make them more complex. As always, you are encouraged to personalize your approach and create an overall system marked by your unique signature.

Healing Check-Ins

It's a good idea to make it a habit to keep track of your energy-healing journey via regular check-ins. These check-ins would work well on a weekly basis, acting as your debrief with yourself, in which you'll summarize how the week went and what might come next. For this purpose and a lot of the exercises already discussed, you are encouraged to keep a journal focused on all the aspects of your energy work.

The end of the workweek or a pleasant Sunday afternoon is generally the best time to have your recap, but other days could work just as well, if not better, depending on the particularities of your schedule. The recap would constitute one part of the check-in, revolving around an analysis of this week's results and observations, made easier by your journal entries. Take note of any changes in how you feel and any problems that might persist despite your efforts in energy healing.

The other part of the check-in is all about figuring out your next steps and addressing your fundamental needs. Use your introspection, intuition, and previous results to figure out what your body, mind, and spirit need to feel healthy and vibrant. The answer doesn't always have to be a specific energy ritual. It can also be a lifestyle change or a new, healthy habit. You must also clearly understand the beliefs, thoughts, and emotional states you need to release or embrace.

The baggage you must get rid of and the new, healthy perspectives you want to adopt hold the key to your energetic and emotional balance. Have this friendly but sincere chat with yourself once a week, and figure out what you need to do to attain inner peace and reconnect with your higher self. You won't always like the answers, and being honest with yourself can be quite difficult, but it's the only way to carve out your path forward.

Morning Energy Alignment

The best way to align your energy before you take on the day is to choose your favorite ritual and do it before you prepare the rest of your morning routine. The preferred ritual is the one that strikes a balance between practicality and tangible benefit. Exercises that focus on centering and grounding tend to work particularly well in the morning, especially if you have the time and space for a few moments of tranquility without distractions.

If you have the luxury to take things outside, an outdoor grounding ritual in the morning will be incredibly energizing. Still, indoor grounding will work just as well if you focus and visualize with enough intention behind it. The important thing is that you conduct your morning grounding ritual in a quiet place where you can have a few undisturbed minutes. As discussed earlier, plant your feet comfortably on the ground, close your eyes, and visualize your preferred mental image of grounding.

Picture the growth of roots from your feet or a flow of vibrant light energy back and forth between your feet and the ground. Focus on the idea of anchoring your energy firmly in the ground beneath your feet, providing the stability and presence that you need to carry out the tasks of the day. Absorb this stabilizing energy from the ground as you breathe deeply and let your mind drift to encouraging thoughts that make daily challenges easier. Imagine yourself walking firmly through whatever comes later, drawing strength from the intimate connection between your energy and that of the earth beneath you.

Morning Breathwork

Breathwork is always a great, rejuvenating way to start your day. Refer to the various breathwork methods you've learned about earlier and choose the one that you feel fits best into your typical morning. It's a good idea to aim for ones that don't strain your body too much and enable you to get the most oxygen quickly. Breathwork methods that emphasize smooth, gentle, and deep breathing will feel good in the morning because they'll encourage consistent airflow and help your heart reach its optimal rhythm first thing in the morning.

One of the best choices is a simple 4-4-4 breathing pattern because it requires little force for most regular practitioners and ensures that you're inhaling just as much air as you're inhaling. It also allows the same interval for your lungs and body to process and diffuse the oxygen evenly. You could also combine your preferred breathwork technique with some basic stretching or gentle yoga poses to enhance circulation and muscle activation. Whatever combination you prefer, it will help you make the most of the energy you've stored during your sleep. That's why it's important to engage in activities after you wake up. Lazy mornings are sometimes the right choice on an emotional level, but they'll dissipate some of your energy into nothing and can make you more sluggish for the rest of the day.

Chakra Tune-Up

Another great way to start your day is to meditate on your chakras, thus reinforcing your connection to them and the awareness of their presence. If you have the time, you can start each morning with a basic chakra scan, visualizing your chakras in their respective places and colors, glowing brightly in your body. The idea is to start the day with a reminder of where your chakras are and what they're doing, placing this thought in the back of your mind as you face the rest of your day. Reconnecting with your chakras is a good daily exercise, but if your schedule isn't too accommodating, it's enough to just start your week that way.

On top of a chakra scan, you can meditate on the light of the morning sun at your window, visualizing it as a stream of fresh morning energy that you'll absorb into your chakra system. It's easy enough to feel energized when you're sitting calmly in sunlight after waking up, but you should focus on the healing properties of this energy with regard to your chakras. Use that light energy and direct it through your chakras as you would in other exercises.

Set an intention that revolves around taking a piece of the sun's new energy while the day is young, accumulating it in your chakras, and carrying it for the rest of the day. Keep the exercise brief and to the point, and see it as a quick chakra tune-up meant to encourage the flow of your energy in the same way a coffee encourages your brain to accelerate after waking up.

Daily Affirmations

If you can make it a habit to start your day with an affirmation, this can be an excellent way to get your mind right before you're even out of bed. It might be a bit difficult to train your mind to automatically fixate on a specific thought as soon as you open your eyes, but it's possible with enough practice and some basic preparation in the evening. You can use your journal to come up with a few different affirmations, one for each morning of the week. Consider the following examples as a general guideline:

- *"I am grounded, balanced, and full of positive energy."*
- *"I attract peace, abundance, and joy."*
- *"I am centered with my energy flowing freely."*
- *"I am synchronized with all there is, and my vibrations are balanced."*

As you fall asleep, set a strong intention to remember such an affirmation and utter it to yourself first thing in the morning, and you might be able to remember it after a few tries. Eventually, it will become a habit to encourage yourself in this way as you get out of bed. If your affirmation is the first thing that pops into your mind, it will be a powerful energy boost in the morning, but it will still provide a lot of benefits – even if it comes a bit later.

You can repeat your preferred affirmations as you engage in breathwork or meditation or while you're going about the usual minutia of your morning routine. What matters is that you keep your intention in your mind and truly reflect on your affirmations instead of just uttering them mechanically as a force of habit. This is why it's best to create your own, highly personal affirmations that you find relatable because they come from deep inside.

Mindfulness in Everyday Tasks

Basic mindfulness can fit into virtually any activity, especially in the morning when the tasks at hand don't require that much investment. Preparing breakfast, taking a shower, washing your face, making coffee, or brushing your teeth are all minor tasks that leave a lot of room for mindfulness. They provide an opportunity to ground yourself in the present moment and center your thoughts without having to worry about the intricate details of what you're doing at the time.

The convenience of mindfulness goes well beyond morning routines, of course. You should try to incorporate it into your lunch breaks and other times when you get a bit of time for yourself at any point in the day. Infuse mindfulness into as many mundane tasks as possible, but use it when you're merely resting. To keep things simple and practical, use the most basic techniques, such as mindful breathing.

For instance, when you're walking or washing your dishes, your mind might normally drift to thoughts that have to do with the task at hand. These can also be moments when your mind shifts to negative thoughts, as walking or washing dishes doesn't require much mental power and focus. When you're stressed out and riddled with worries, these are the moments when your mind will usually start focusing on such negativity.

Instead, try to do a quick 5-4-3-2-1 exercise as an intro to get you centered and focused on the present moment. Once you're present, switch your focus to your breathing. Don't try to breathe a certain way or alter your breathing pattern. Simply observe the pattern and be a witness to it, letting the action of breath occupy your mind and anchor it in the present. Foster an awareness of each step as you walk, making all other concerns fade away in your mind. Beyond mindfulness in tasks, try to have at least one or two breathwork pauses at various points in the day to center, reset, and recharge your energy.

Bless Your Food and Drink

Since food is an essential part of your everyday routine, not to mention a life-sustaining necessity, it offers plenty of opportunities to tinker with your energy. Paying more attention to the food you prepare or consume can direct some of your energy toward this physical form of sustenance. Taking a few moments to bless your food and drink with healing intentions can constitute a pleasant little ritual that energizes the things you eat and drink and fosters physical and emotional wellness.

Of course, you should use whatever ritual structure you feel is most appropriate. Elements of most mainline religions focus quite a bit on food, so you can use that as a foundation to build your own special rituals with regard to food. The simplest way to infuse your food with positive intention is to recite a prayer or some other kind of verbal blessing directed at the food as you're about to eat. You can do the same with individual ingredients if you frequently partake in cooking.

Additionally, you can include healing or sacred herbs in your recipes where applicable to give your intentions some physical backing. Refer to earlier discussions about herbs as they relate to your chakras and overall energy, finding those that are edible and suited to your tastes. You can also replace regular kitchen salt with kinds that are more conducive to energy healing. Construct your tailored personal system of food preparation that emphasizes its spiritual aspects and turn the whole thing into an exercise in spiritual awareness. If you create a meaningful ritual around your food, you might find that your meals are more enjoyable instead of being something you do mechanically. The right ingredients and even a positive attitude can contribute to better digestion, too.

Energy Healing Glossary for Quick Reference

To tie things off, this bonus chapter will provide a basic glossary of various terms and concepts found in energy healing, with appropriate definitions. It will serve as a quick yet fairly detailed recap of a lot of the concepts you've learned about, presented in a comprehensive format well-suited for reference on the fly. If you find yourself in the middle of a meditation ritual or some other exercise and can't quite remember some bit of information, keep this summary handy. It will allow you to swiftly refresh your understanding of these ideas and get right back to your exercise without sifting through chapters and pages.

Aromatherapy

An approach to energy healing that relies on activating your sense of smell as a channel through which you'll absorb healing energy. This technique is best used to enhance other rituals or foster a healing atmosphere throughout your home or working spaces for prolonged periods of time. Use aromatherapy to improve your healing baths, empower meditation, and encourage visualization exercises that can benefit from scents. Consider the following tools and sources as your scent mediums:

- Essential oils
- Diffusers
- Incense sticks
- Smudging herbs
- Carrier oils
- Flowers and plants
- Steam
- Topical solutions
- Healing bath products
- Natural outdoor areas

Aura

Often used interchangeably with energy field, energy body, or bioenergy, your aura is your personal energy signature that projects around the contours of your body and reflects a lot about you. The aura itself doesn't really act as a protective layer, but it can influence various outcomes in the physical world. It can attract or turn away energies, people, fortune, circumstances, and more. In the spiritual realm, where energies constantly interact, your aura represents you as an entity. This personal energy field can be strengthened, weakened, and altered due to external stimuli or your own actions, such as meditation, visualization, breathwork, and other spiritual practices.

Auric Layer

Seven distinct layers make up your aura, stacked on top of each other and extending outward from your body in a specific order. They also correspond to chakras and can be seen as conduits of energy that enable your aura and chakras to communicate with each other. For this reason, the aura with its layers is sometimes regarded as embodying your chakra system. The state of your chakras will often be reflected in your auric layers, affecting the appearance, strength, and nature of your aura as a whole. Each layer also governs specific aspects of you as a person and entity, both in a spiritual and physical sense. Refer to the chart below for a quick refresher on how your aura layers are ordered and what some of their aspects are.

Order	Layer name	Associated aspect	Related chakra
First	Physical	All things physical	Root
Second	Emotional	Emotions	Sacral
Third	Mental	Thoughts, beliefs	Solar plexus
Fourth	Astral	The bridge between the physical and spiritual	Heart
Fifth	Etheric	Spiritual blueprint of the body	Throat

Order	Layer name	Associated aspect	Related chakra
Sixth	Celestial	Intuition, wisdom	Third eye
Seventh	Causal	Enlightenment, higher spirituality	Crown

Ayurveda

Occasionally used as a synonym for energy healing in some circles, Ayurveda refers to a body of Indian teachings and practices in traditional or alternative medicine. Ayurveda can be a powerful tradition to study if you want to dive into energy healing at even greater depths, particularly through a multi-millennium lens of well-established Eastern traditions. Like all energy healing approaches, Ayurveda seeks to establish a balance of body, mind, and spirit in a truly holistic approach to wellness. It's an extensive field of study that you can spend years learning about if you decide to dive in. Ayurveda emphasizes the interconnectedness of all there is and uses these invisible cords to heal.

Chakra

Seven crucial nodes are aligned along your spinal column in a specific order. These vortexes of energy are places where your energy converges and passes through, which makes them the focal point of many energy-related exercises. The objective is to keep chakras clear so that energy can flow freely. In your many visualizations and meditations, consult the chart below for a quick rundown on the order, names, and various essential associations for each chakra.

Order	Sanskrit Name	Colloquial Name	Location	Chant	Color	Element
First	Muladhara	Root	Tailbone	Lam	Red	Earth
Second	Svadhishthana	Sacral	Lower abdomen	Vam	Orange	Water
Third	Manipura	Solar plexus	Upper abdomen	Ram	Yellow	Fire

Order	Sanskrit Name	Colloquial Name	Location	Chant	Color	Element
Fourth	Anahata	Heart	Heart area	Yam	Green	Air
Fifth	Vishuddha	Throat	Throat	Ham	Blue	Space / ether
Sixth	Ajna	Third eye	Forehead / brow	Om	Indigo	Light / none
Seventh	Sahastrara	Crown	Top of head	Ah	Violet / white	None

Chant

Simplistic, guttural sounds that vibrate at frequencies appropriate for individual chakras. The seven main chants are commonly used in meditation and are important tools for communicating with your chakras, encouraging their activation, clearing them, focusing energy and thoughts, and much more. Chants are highly applicable and are a welcome addition to many energy rituals, so use them freely and appropriately. They will interfere with breathwork, however, so they are best used in meditation, journeying, visualization, and other techniques that rely on mental focus.

Energy Body

Frequently used as an alternative term for your aura, but described somewhat differently in certain traditions. Your energy body is an energetic projection of the self in the realm of spirits and energies. It consists of layers, often referred to as the subtle bodies, similar to the aura concept. You can use this terminology in place of the aura if you find the words more conducive to meditating on energy and visualizing it. Think of your energy body as an ethereal alter ego made up of pure life force. It's a second spiritual body that you must take care of just as your physical one.

Energy Shielding

Energy shielding is a wide body of different practices that fall under the concept of spiritual protection. Through various techniques, it seeks to project an added layer or extra energy field around your aura, chakras, and other integral parts of your energy. It's primarily used to fight back against negative energies, psychic attacks, spiritual interference, malice, and other negative forces that could drain or weaken your energy. Energy shielding relies primarily on visualization, but it also works through props like salt, smudge kits, crystals, and various other tools that have protective attributes.

Grounding

Grounding is the practice of quickly and effectively *grounding* yourself in the present moment and space. It's about mental recall, where you can shift your thoughts on command, relieve your mind of stress, and attain focus. It's commonly used when you're feeling unstable or shaken by external influences or inner turmoil. Grounding is a simple technique that comes in various forms and provides momentary or prolonged senses of stability and strength physically, emotionally, and mentally. Grounding benefits from outdoor practice, but it can also be done indoors or on the fly with simplified visualization techniques. The mental objective is to foster a sense of connection to the earth and draw strength and peace from the thought.

Journeying

This is a more complex level of deep visualization. Inner journeys are visualization exercises that benefit from deeper meditation, and they consist of visual journeys through places, scenarios, and spiritual interactions. While it plays a prominent role in energy healing, visualized journeying is especially important for spiritual communication in traditions like shamanism. Shamans induce states of trance through sophisticated mental and spiritual effort, in which they interact with spiritual entities or mentally travel to sacred places in the pursuit of wisdom and enlightenment.

Mindfulness

As its name suggests, mindfulness is all about being mindful – of the current moment, the task at hand, and the place you're in. It's a technique aimed at fostering an enhanced sense of presence, which provides calm, focus, and command over your attention span. It enables the practitioner to block out distractions or stress and remain stably focused on whatever they're doing at a given moment. Mindfulness is practiced on many levels of complexity, with the most common approach being mindful breathing. Unlike strict breathwork, mindful breathing is about observing, not controlling your breaths. The goal is to use one's natural breathing pattern as an object of focus and grounding, but many other such objects can be used instead of breathing.

Negativity

Negativity or negative energy is a broad term that represents all those external energy influences that you want to avoid. It comes from a great variety of sources and takes on many forms, but all these forms are detrimental to your energy in some way. Negative energy leads to debilitating states of mind, spiritual lethargy, and even physical symptoms in serious cases. Deflecting such energy or cleansing it is a major point of focus for all manner of spiritual and energy work. Negative energy can be both internal and external, and some of its more infamous forms include curses, hexes, and general toxicity.

Prana

A unifying Sanskrit term that simply refers to an essential life force or energy that fuels the vitality of all that lives in the universe. Prana is the name of the game in all practices related to energy work. It's what you'll be looking for: inviting in, using, shaping, and absorbing for healing. Prana flows through all living creatures, and the goal of energy work is to remove any and all obstacles that might stand in its way. Unfortunately, life can create many such obstacles, and that's where energy healing traditions come into play.

Pranayama

The Sanskrit synonym for breathwork is used widely in all things related to yoga. Pranayama is defined as breath control aimed at capturing Prana and using it for your benefit on the physical, emotional, and spiritual levels. It has its place in energy healing, traditional medicine, meditation, yoga, martial arts, and many other circles. You can use the word fully interchangeably with breathwork and favor it if you want to approach energy healing primarily through Indian traditions with a more authentic feel. Breathwork is one of the key components in most rituals discussed in the book, which makes pranayama one of the most important practices to master. The bullet points below will list some of the most popular forms of Pranayama.

- Nadi Shodhana

- Bhastrika

- Kapalabhati

- Ujjayi

- Bhramari

- Kumbhaka

Qi

A concept very similar to that of Prana, Qi originates in ancient Chinese traditions and describes the same life energy that permeates all beings. Just like Prana, your Qi is something that should flow freely and be in balance, which can be done through energy work, spiritualism, traditional medicine, and other approaches. The concept of Qi also finds its place in martial arts, which take a holistic approach to strength and the art of combat. In Chinese traditions, Qi is often considered a material form of energy, which means it's a substance with energetic attributes.

Reiki

Reiki is a more recent body of practices aimed at energy healing. It draws inspiration from Eastern traditions in energy work and medicine. Reiki comes from Japan and was first devised in the early 20th century before arriving in the United States a few decades later. In the teachings of Reiki, the universal energy of life is referred to as Rei. As with other approaches to energy healing, Reiki teaches that this energy can be harnessed and channeled for the purpose of healing the human body. Reiki professionals commonly manipulate life energy through their hands via touch or proximity.

Smudging

Smudging relies on burning sacred herbs like white sage to cleanse spaces, people, and objects of negative energy. It's a welcome tool in various rituals as an additional layer of protection and cleansing, but it can also help you cleanse other props and prepare them for rituals that might not involve smudging. You can use your smudge kit to clear crystals, foster a positive atmosphere at home, prepare your meditation space for an exercise, and much more. With the right smudging kit, it will be a very easy and applicable ritual that you can use whenever you feel the need.

Sound Therapy

You can view sound therapy as the auditory version of aromatherapy. With that said, sound therapy has the potential to be much more powerful in energy work because it makes use of highly observable vibrations that directly affect your sensory input. Scent/smell is a sense, too, but sound is vibration manifest. What your sound therapy will look like depends on the kind of ritual you're using, the result you're seeking, your mindset, the environment, and much more. Sound can be used as the central point of a ritual, but it can also provide a powerful backdrop at the appropriate volume, making an excellent addition to all manner of seemingly unrelated energy practices.

Vibration

Everything in the universe, be it a sound, object, thought, person, or plant, has a particular vibrating frequency. Frequencies can change depending on the underlying energy state, which can be the goal of certain energy work techniques or a symptom of an energy problem. Because of their omnipresence, vibrations are important in energy healing. Many of the rituals and techniques discussed in this book will affect vibrations in some way or produce their own, depending on the sounds, props, and thoughts you use. As popular wisdom has long known, there are good and bad vibrations, and the good ones are those that are natural, balanced, and in sync.

Visualization

The essential technique of visualization is one of the most important instruments in your energy healing toolset. It simply means setting an intention and using the eye of your mind to meditate on that intention with mental intensity and in detail until that intention can manifest. You can visualize forms of energy, vibrations, objects, and outcomes. Visualizing an outcome in whatever you are pursuing helps you stay focused and shrug off any setbacks or interference in the pursuit of that goal. The depth and intensity of your visualizations will depend on the amount of effort you put into your rituals and mental techniques.

Conclusion

The important point to take home is that achieving energetic balance and spiritual peace means adopting a particular mentality and lifestyle. It's not about mechanically conducting a certain ritual for a set amount of repetitions and waiting for a miracle. In that, energy work differs from physical exercise. What makes or breaks an energy ritual such as meditation and visualization is the power and focus of the intention behind it. Carrying out the exercises correctly is still important, of course, but success will depend in great part on where you are mentally.

Using the knowledge you've gathered across the preceding chapters, you'll have a lot of tools at your disposal. At the end of the day, you should strive to create your own personalized approach to energy healing that works best for you. A lot of the exercises, tools, and advice provided in this book are at least somewhat modular, allowing for a degree of experimentation and improvisation. You should play around with all of them and use a journal to keep a meticulous record of the results. Adjust them accordingly and try out different routines that fit into your lifestyle, but do make lifestyle changes when you have to.

Another thing to remember is that healing can take time and considerable effort. Modern life is filled with stress and all manner of negativity that can accumulate for years and even decades before an individual realizes that they need a spiritual change. If your energy healing journey doesn't yield results in the short term, you mustn't assume that living a life of balance and peace is something beyond your reach. With enough commitment and practice in energy work, you can achieve inner peace and a profound, holistic sense of well-being regardless of your current situation.

In many ways, balancing your energy is like returning to your natural state of being or coming home since a healthy energy body is one that's tuned into the energy of the universe. To align your chakras and strengthen your aura is to reassert your natural position in a much wider system of energy. It's a system where you and every other living creature belong and play an essential part. Returning to that place of belonging and harmony within the self and within one big everything is what energy healing is all about. The stresses and disappointments of material life can sometimes make you forget about that place, but meditation and spiritual work will help you remember.

If you enjoyed this book, I'd greatly appreciate a review on Amazon because it helps me to create more books that people want. It would mean a lot to hear from you.

To leave a review:

1. Open your camera app.
2. Point your mobile device at the QR code.
3. The review page will appear in your web browser.

Thanks for your support!

MARI SILVA
The
Seven
Chakras
A GUIDE TO THE ROOT, SACRAL,
SOLAR PLEXUS, HEART, THROAT,
THIRD EYE, AND CROWN CHAKRA

Your Free Gift
(only available for a limited time)

Thanks for getting this book! If you want to learn more about various spirituality topics, then join Mari Silva's community and get a free guided meditation MP3 for awakening your third eye. This guided meditation mp3 is designed to open and strengthen ones third eye so you can experience a higher state of consciousness. Simply visit the link below the image to get started.

https://spiritualityspot.com/meditation

Or, Scan the QR code!

References

Beckman, H. (2024, October 31). *Exploring the History and Origins of Energy Healing - The Argyle Oracle*. The Argyle Oracle - the Argyle Oracle. https://argyleoracle.com.au/exploring-the-history-and-origins-of-energy-healing/

Body & Soul Ascension Mastery. (2023, April 24). *Energy Frequency and Spiritual Vibration Chart: A Comprehensive Guide*. Body&Soul Ascension. https://www.bodyandsoulascension.com/post/energy-frequency-and-spiritual-vibration-chart-a-comprehensive-guide

Burgin, T. (2022, January 30). *24 Ways to Clear Negative Energy From Your Body and Home*. Yoga Basics. https://www.yogabasics.com/connect/yoga-blog/clear-negative-energy/

Cronkleton, E., & Walters, O. (2022, March 16). *Alternate Nostril Breathing: Benefits, How To, and More*. Healthline. https://www.healthline.com/health/alternate-nostril-breathing

Dave. (2018, June 12). *Read My Aura: How to See Your Chakras & Check Your Aura*. Aura Camera. https://aura.net/how-to-see-your-chakras/

Dr. Liz. (2024, May 7). *Balancing Your Chakras with Essential Oils - Aluminate Life*. Aluminate Life. https://aluminatelife.com/balancing-your-chakras-with-essential-oils/

Gomez, L. G. (5 C.E., November). *The Seven Chakras and Essential Oils to Align Them*. Nikura. https://nikura.com/blogs/living-well/the-seven-chakras-and-essential-oils-to-align-them

Gotter, A. (2017, March 23). *Box Breathing*. Healthline. https://www.healthline.com/health/box-breathing#benefits

Grounds, L. (2023, June 26). *The Power of Vibration*. Medium. https://medium.com/@lesliegrounds/the-power-of-vibration-c359d961291f6

Harrison, T. (2021, February 15). *Understanding The Seven Layers Of The Human Aura*. The Minds Journal. https://www.themindsjournal.com/layers-of-human-aura/

Harvard Health Publishing. (2016, March 10). *Learning Diaphragmatic Breathing*. Harvard Health. https://www.health.harvard.edu/healthbeat/learning-diaphragmatic-breathing

Holland, K. (2018, December 3). *Are Auras Real? 15 FAQs About Color, Meaning, More*. Healthline. https://www.healthline.com/health/what-is-an-aura

Jain, R. (2019, June 13). *What are the 7 Chakras? A Guide of the Energy Centers and their Effects*. Arhanta Yoga Ashram. https://www.arhantayoga.org/blog/7-chakras-introduction-energy-centers-effect/

Jessika. (2024). *Meditation: San Jose Gnostic Order of Christ: Auric Egg Exercise*. Gnostic.org. https://gnostic.org/meditations/meditationsitting/pages/meditation3how.htm

Johansson, N. (2019, March 14). *How to do Kumbhaka Pranayama - Full Breath Retention*. Yogateket. https://www.yogateket.com/blog/how-to-do-kumbhaka-pranayama-full-breath-retention

Mendez, D. (2024, January 18). *Understanding Negative Energy: Sources, Effects, And How To Clear And Protect Yourself – YogaDura*. Yogadura.com. https://yogadura.com/what-is-negative-energy/

Mitali. (2025, April 12). *5-Minute Mindfulness: Quick Ways to Reset Your Day*. Timeslife. https://timeslife.com/life-hacks/5-minute-mindfulness-quick-ways-to-reset-your-day/articleshow/120200489.html

Mosunic, C. (2023, September 12). *5, 4, 3, 2, 1 – – A Simple Grounding Exercise to Calm Anxiety*. Calm Blog. https://www.calm.com/blog/5-4-3-2-1-a-simple-exercise-to-calm-the-mind

Nast, C. (2021, September 16). *Everyone's Talking About Vibrational Frequency, but Can It Actually Improve Your Spiritual Wellbeing?* Glamour UK. https://www.glamourmagazine.co.uk/article/vibrational-frequency

Polona. (2021, June 10). *6 Ways to Protect Your Aura - Energetic Field - Shewolfka*. Shewolfka. https://shewolfka.com/how-to-protect-your-aura-and-energetic-field/

Preston, C. (13 C.E., January). *Chakra Crystals: The Best Crystals for Each Chakra*. Almanacsupplyco.com. https://almanacsupplyco.com/blogs/articles/the-best-crystals-for-each-chakra

Psychic Jenna. (2025, May 12). *A Complete Guide to Psychic Protection and Psychic Self-Defense*. Https://Www.psychicsource.com. https://www.psychicsource.com/article/other-psychic-topics/a-complete-guide-to-psychic-protection-and-psychic-self-defense/24918

Quest, P. (2002, December). *Auras and Chakras*. Reiki.

https://www.reiki.org/articles/auras-and-chakras

Quinn, J. (2021, July 21). *Aura 101: Everything You Need to Know About the Aura*. Sunday Edit. https://edit.sundayriley.com/aura-101-everything-you-need-to-know-about-the-aura/

Rivers, A. (2023, August 8). *Evaluating Energetic Flow: How to Test Chakras*. Chakraseeker.com. https://chakraseeker.com/how-to-test-chakras/

Saka, G. (2023, January 6). *Herbs for the Chakras*. Organic India. https://www.organicindiausa.com/blog/herbs-for-the-chakras/

Stanborough, R. J. (2020, November 13). *What is vibrational energy? Definition, benefits & more*. Healthline. https://www.healthline.com/health/vibrational-energy

Stelter, G. (2016, October 4). *A Beginner's Guide to the 7 Chakras and Their Meanings*. Healthline; Healthline Media. https://www.healthline.com/health/fitness-exercise/7-chakras

Tanaaz. (2016, April 26). *The 7 Layers of Your Aura*. Forever Conscious. https://foreverconscious.com/7-layers-aura

The Enlightenment Journey. (2024, August 10). *How To Strengthen Your Aura For Positive Energy*. The Enlightenment Journey. https://theenlightenmentjourney.com/how-to-strengthen-your-aura-for-positive-energy/

The Manifestation Collective. (2021, February 2). *How To Cleanse And Charge Your Crystals As A Beginner*. The Manifestation Collective. https://themanifestationcollective.co/how-cleanse-charge-crystals-beginner/

The Wellness Nest. (2020, July 24). *How To Use Crystals + How To Cleanse Your Crystals*. The Wellness Nest | Melbourne Myotherapist. https://www.thewellnessnest.com.au/blog/how-to-use-crystals

WebMD Editorial Contributor, & Bhandari, S. (2022, December 11). *Signs of Negative Energy*. WebMD. https://www.webmd.com/balance/signs-negative-energy

WebMD Editorial Contributors. (2021, June 28). *What Are Chakras?* WebMD. https://www.webmd.com/balance/what-are-chakras

Welch, A. (2023, July 11). *What Is Energy Healing?* EverydayHealth.com. https://www.everydayhealth.com/integrative-health/energy-healing/guide/

Zering, K. (2023, April 25). *History of Energy Healing - Energy Rapport™ with Kathy Zering*. Energy Rapport™ with Kathy Zering. https://energyrapport.com/the-history-of-energy-healing-from-ancient-times-to-modern-practice/

Zoldan, R. J. (2020). *Your 7 Chakras, Explained— – Plus, How to Tell if They're Blocked*. Well+Good. https://www.wellandgood.com/lifestyle/what-are-chakras

Zove, M. (2023, October 20). *Protect Your Home from Negative Energy: A Complete Guide to Rituals.* Your Soul Time®; Your Soul Time®. https://www.yoursoultime.com/blogs/nasveti/zascitite-svoj-dom-pred-negativno-energijo-celovit-vodic-ritualov

Image Sources

1   Designed by Freepik. https://www.freepik.com/free-photo/side-view-adult-meditating-with-light_34877527.htm#fromView=search&page=1&position=10&uuid=3a83eaea-ba81-4641-9abc-9d7d4465fad2&query=energy+healing

2   Photo by Meagan Carsience on Unsplash https://unsplash.com/photos/a-blurry-image-of-a-red-object-in-the-dark-txThZOwDrCs

3   Photo by Mikhail Nilov: https://www.pexels.com/photo/woman-in-yellow-jacket-and-blue-denim-jeans-sitting-on-blue-round-inflatable-ring-6931924/

4   Photo by cottonbro studio: https://www.pexels.com/photo/man-in-black-shorts-sitting-on-floor-4325466/

5   Designed by Freepik. https://www.freepik.com/free-photo/woman-maintaining-asana-while-chakra-points-are-aligned_21794869.htm#fromView=search&page=1&position=13&uuid=3a83eaea-ba81-4641-9abc-9d7d4465fad2&query=energy+healing

6   Image by Peter Lomas from Pixabay https://pixabay.com/illustrations/root-chakra-energy-chi-spiritual-2533091/

7   Image by Peter Lomas from Pixabay https://pixabay.com/illustrations/sacral-chakra-energy-chi-spiritual-2533094/

8   Image by Peter Lomas from Pixabay https://pixabay.com/illustrations/solar-chakra-chi-energy-spiritual-2533097/

9   Image by Peter Lomas from Pixabay https://pixabay.com/illustrations/heart-chakra-energy-chi-spiritual-2533104/

10 Image by Peter Lomas from Pixabay https://pixabay.com/illustrations/throat-chakra-chi-energy-spiritual-2533108/

11 Image by Peter Lomas from Pixabay https://pixabay.com/illustrations/brow-chakra-energy-chi-spiritual-2533110/

12 Image by Peter Lomas from Pixabay https://pixabay.com/illustrations/crown-chakra-energy-chi-spiritual-2533113/

13 Image by Doreen Sawitza from Pixabay https://pixabay.com/illustrations/wailpaper-aura-meditation-emotion-2111346/

14 Image by Karin Henseler from Pixabay https://pixabay.com/illustrations/aura-chakra-to-dye-esoteric-center-1079746/

15 Photo by christopher lemercier on Unsplash https://unsplash.com/photos/man-sitting-on-chair-covering-his-eyes-12yvdCiLaVE

16 Photo by Mikhail Nilov: https://www.pexels.com/photo/a-woman-trying-alternative-6944697/

17 Eurico Zimbres, CC BY-SA 2.5 <https://creativecommons.org/licenses/by-sa/2.5>, via Wikimedia Commons https://commons.wikimedia.org/wiki/File:Gypsum_selenite.jpg

18 Photo by Christin Hume on Unsplash https://unsplash.com/photos/person-holding-amber-glass-bottle-0MoF-Fe0w0A

19 sgrantarch, Attribution-NonCommercial-ShareAlike 2.0 Generic, CC BY-NC-SA 2.0 < https://creativecommons.org/licenses/by-nc-sa/2.0/deed.en> https://www.flickr.com/photos/sgrantarch/3570643286

20 Photo by KATRIN BOLOVTSOVA: https://www.pexels.com/photo/a-burning-sage-on-a-shell-with-pearls-6766465/

21 Timon Jähnert, CC BY 2.0 <https://creativecommons.org/licenses/by/2.0>, via Wikimedia Commons https://commons.wikimedia.org/wiki/File:Black_Tourmaline_with_Quartz_(48340709947).jpg

22 Photo by karla munoz rosas: https://www.pexels.com/photo/aromatherapy-diffuser-with-essential-oils-display-29146991/

23 Image by vined mind from Pixabay https://pixabay.com/photos/woman-girl-meditate-relax-calm-8563442/

24 Photo by cottonbro studio: https://www.pexels.com/photo/man-in-black-crew-neck-t-shirt-sitting-on-brown-sofa-4553272/

25 Photo by Orange Ocean: https://www.pexels.com/photo/woman-reading-by-tranquil-lotus-pond-outdoors-32251049/

26 Photo by Pixabay: https://www.pexels.com/photo/waterfalls-during-daytime-62627/

27 Photo by James Wheeler: https://www.pexels.com/photo/crop-field-under-rainbow-and-cloudy-skies-at-dayime-1542495/

28 Photo by Designecologist: https://www.pexels.com/photo/person-holding-clear-glass-jar-905894/

29 Photo by monicore: https://www.pexels.com/photo/close-up-photo-of-himalayan-salt-2624400/

30 Photo by Andre Furtado: https://www.pexels.com/photo/woman-surrounded-by-sunflowers-1263986/